RENEWING BUSINESS TENANCIES

Third edition

Graham Fife MA (Oxon), Solicitor, Manches LLP

Brian Hilditch LLB (Hons), Solicitor, Manches LLP

JORDANS

2005

Published by
Jordan Publishing Limited
21 St Thomas Street
Bristol BS1 6JS

Reprinted September 2005

British Library Cataloguing-in-Publication Data
A catalogue record for this book is available from the British Library.

ISBN 0 85308 843 8

Typeset by MFK-Mendip, Frome, Somerset
Printed in Great Britain by Antony Rowe Limited

PREFACE

In 2004, business tenancies underwent the most significant reform since Part II of the Landlord and Tenant Act 1954 itself. The regime for the renewal of such tenancies was radically altered by the Regulatory Reform (Business Tenancies) (England and Wales) Order 2003.

Where the ball started rolling, by the service of a Section 25 Notice or a Section 26 Request, on or after 1 June 2004:

–   the landlord needs to include its proposals for the new tenancy in its Section 25 Notice;
–   the tenant does not need to serve a counter notice;
–   either the landlord or the tenant can make the court application (and if the landlord objects to renewal, it can apply for an order that the tenancy is terminated without renewal);
–   the old time limits for making a court application have been scrapped; the application can be made at any time up to the specified termination date of the old tenancy and there is now a statutory basis for extending even that time limit by agreement;
–   either the landlord or the tenant can apply for interim rent, which will be calculated in one of many new ways.

Though much has changed, much has also remained the same. In particular, the seven statutory grounds on which a landlord may object to renewal have not changed, nor the basis on which the court would fix the terms of the new tenancy and the rent payable under the new tenancy.

Where the ball started rolling, by the service of a Section 25 Notice or a Section 26 Request, on or before 31 May 2004, the old law will continue to apply.

The purpose of this book remains to provide a simple practical guide to the old law and the new law, both for property lawyers and for the landlords and tenants directly affected and their other professional advisers. To this end, we have retained the format used in the previous two editions of statement followed by comment, with practical tips for both landlords and tenants.

We trust you will find this third edition useful and, as always, would welcome any comments and suggestions for inclusion in any future editions.

We would like to thank our colleagues at Manches LLP for their suggestions and support over the years, and in particular the members of the Property Litigation Team, past and present.

The law is stated as at January 2005.

Graham Fife
Brian Hilditch
Manches LLP
January 2005

CONTENTS

Preface   v
Table of Cases   xi
Table of Statutes   xvii
Table of Statutory Instruments   xix

Chapter 1   THE STATUTORY TENANCY UNDER THE
             LANDLORD AND TENANT ACT 1954, PART II   1
             1.1   Definitions   1
             1.2   Transitional provisions   1
             1.3   The protection in outline   1
             1.4   What is a business tenancy?   2
             1.5   Exclusions from the Act   2
             1.6   Contracting out   3

Chapter 2   THE LANDLORD'S POSITION   5
             2.1   Initial considerations   5
             2.2   Section 40 Notice   6
             2.3   Section 25 Notice   7
             2.4   Timing and tactics   9
             2.5   New options for landlords: order for termination
                    or apply itself for new lease   10
             2.6   Some cases on validity   11
             2.7   Methods of service   14
             2.8   The competent landlord   15
             2.9   Consequences of unlawful assignment   18
             2.10   Group occupation and trustee provisions   18
             2.11   Partnerships: assignment without assignment   20
             2.12   The insolvent landlord   20

Chapter 3   THE TENANT'S POSITION   23
             3.1   Tenant's request for a new tenancy under
                    section 26   23
             3.2   Tenant's tactics   24
             3.3   Section 26 and tenant's break clauses   25
             3.4   Section 25 Notice and the tenant   26
             3.5   Tenant's time-limits – warning   26
             3.6   Diary dates for tenant after Section 25 Notice   28
             3.7   Diary dates for tenant after Section 26 Notice   29

3.8	Tenant's response to defective Section 25 Notice	29
3.9	Notices and pending land actions	30

Chapter 4 GROUNDS FOR OPPOSITION — 31

4.1	Permitted grounds	31
4.2	Section 30(1)(f): intention to demolish or reconstruct	32
4.3	Section 30(1)(g): intention to occupy	35

Chapter 5 THE NEW LEASE: THE PROPERTY AND TERMS — 39

5.1	The property comprised in the new lease	39
5.2	Variation of terms	39
5.3	Duration and landlord's break clauses	40
5.4	Guarantors	42
5.5	Fixing the initial rent	42
5.6	Rent review	43
5.7	Repairs, reinstatement and alterations	45
5.8	Impact of the Landlord and Tenant (Covenants) Act 1995	46
5.9	Essential terms: advice for tenants	50
5.10	Costs of the new lease	52

Chapter 6 THE NEW COURT PROCEDURES — 55

6.1	Control in the hands of the court	55
6.2	High Court or county court	56
6.3	Which county court?	57
6.4	The application	57
6.5	Responding to the application	61
6.6	Interim rent	63
6.7	Fixing a date for the first hearing	65
6.8	Agreeing directions	65
6.9	Offers to settle	72
6.10	Costs generally	74
6.11	Court order for the grant of a new tenancy	75
6.12	Alternative dispute resolution: PACT	75

Chapter 7 WITHDRAWAL AND DISCONTINUANCE — 77

7.1	Giving up the property	77
7.2	Section 27(1): pre-emption	77
7.3	Tenant's withdrawal prior to proceedings	77
7.4	Section 27(2): no longer a quarter day notice	77
7.5	Discontinuance	78
7.6	Walking away after contractual expiry date – no longer an option	78

	7.7	Court procedures for discontinuance	79
	7.8	Dilapidations	80
Chapter 8		INTERIM RENT	81
	8.1	Introduction	81
	8.2	Old law: from when does interim rent run?	82
	8.3	New law: from when does interim rent run?	82
	8.4	Old law: principles of calculation	83
	8.5	Will an interim rent under the old law always be below the new rent?	85
	8.6	Old law: does a landlord really want to apply for an interim rent?	86
	8.7	New law: principles of calculation	86
	8.8	New law: are last day rent reviews a dead letter?	89
	8.9	Advice for landlords	90
Chapter 9		DILAPIDATIONS	93
	9.1	Claims for dilapidations	93
	9.2	Redevelopment and claims for dilapidations	93
	9.3	The service charge trap	94
	9.4	Forfeiture on grounds of disrepair	94
Chapter 10		COMPENSATION	95
	10.1	Introduction	95
	10.2	Basis of calculation	95
	10.3	Rating revaluation	98
	10.4	Tax	99
	10.5	Compensation for misrepresentation	99
	10.6	Contracting out	99
Chapter 11		IMPROVEMENTS: SOME COMMENTS ON THE LANDLORD AND TENANT ACT 1927	101
	11.1	Tenant's rights to carry out improvements	101
	11.2	The statutory procedure	101
	11.3	Compensation for improvements	102
Chapter 12		THE TELECOMMUNICATIONS CODE	103
	12.1	Introduction	103
	12.2	Conditions when the Code applies	104
	12.3	Rights under the Code	104
	12.4	Reinstatement under the Code – paragraphs 20 and 21	105
	12.5	Tips for operators	108
	12.6	Tips for occupiers	108

Appendix 1: NOTICES   111
             Landlord's Section 40 Notice – Landlord's Request for
             Information about Occupation and Sub-tenencies   113
             Section 25 Notice – Landlord's Notice Ending a Business
             Tenancy with Proposals for a new one   117
             Section 25 Notice– Landlord's Notice Ending a Business
             Tenancy and Reasons for Refusing a new one   121
             Section 26 Request – Tenant's Request for a New
             Business Tenancy   125
             Tenant's Section 40 Notice – Tenant's Request for
             Information from Landlord or Landlord's Mortgagee
             About Landlord's Interest   129
             Landlord's Section 26 Counter Notice   131

Appendix 2: TIMETABLES UNDER THE NEW LAW   133
             Landlord wishing to terminate tenancy under Landlord
             and Tenant Act 1954, Part II   135
             Tenant wishing to renew (no sub-tenants)   137
             Tenant who has sub-let part and occupies another part
             wishing to renew   139

Appendix 3: CHECKLISTS OF INFORMATION   141
             Acting for landlord serving Section 25 Notice   143
             Acting for landlord who has received Section 26 Request   145
             Acting for tenant intending to serve Section 26 Request   147
             Acting for tenant who has received Section 25 Notice   151

Appendix 4: LANDLORD AND TENANT ACT 1954, PART II   153
             Landlord and Tenant Act 1954, Part II   155

Index   181

TABLE OF CASES

References are to paragraph numbers

Aberdeen Steak House Groups Limited v The Crown Estate Commissioners
[1997] 2 EGLR 107, [1997] 31 EG 101, [1997] NPC 12, CA   4.2
Adams v Green [1978] 2 EGLR 46, CA   5.3
Aly v Aly (1984) 128 SJ 65, (1984) 81 LS Gaz 283, CA   6.4
Amarjee v Barrowfen Properties Ltd [1993] 2 EGLR 133, [1993] 30 EG 98,
Cty Ct   5.6, 8.4
Ambrose v Kaye [2002] 1 EGLR 49, [2002] EWCA Civ 91   4.3
Amica Motors Limited v Colebrook Holdings Limited [1981] 2 EGLR 62   5.3
Artemiou v Procopiou [1966] 1 QB 878, [1965] 3 WLR 1011, [1965] 3 All ER
539   4.3
Artoc Bank & Trust Ltd v Prudential Assurance Co plc [1984] 1 WLR 1181,
[1984] 3 All ER 538, (1984) 271 EG 454   7.7
Arundel Corporation v The Financial Trading Company Limited (2000)
unreported   7.6
Atkinsons v Bettison [1955] 1 WLR 1127, [1955] 3 All ER 340, (1955) 99 SJ 761
                                                                          4.2

Bacchiocchi v Academic Agency Limited [1998] 1 WLR 1313, [1998] 2 All ER
241, [1998] 3 EGLR 157, CA   10.2
Baglarbasi v Deedmethod Ltd [1991] 2 EGLR 71, [1991] 29 EG 137, [1990]
EGCS 155   2.9
Barclays Bank Ltd v Ascott [1961] 1 WLR 717, [1961] 1 All ER 782, (1961) 111
SJ 350   5.4
Barclays Bank plc v Bee [2001] EWCA Civ 1126, [2001] 3 EGLR 41, [2002] 1
WLR 332   2.6
Beanby Estates Limited v Egg Stores (Stamford Hill) Limited [2003] 1 WLR
2064, [2003] EWHC 1252, Ch   2.7
Becker v Hill Street Properties Limited [1990] 2 EGLR 78, [1990] 38 EG 107,
CA   5.3
Betty's Cafes Ltd v Phillips Furnishing Stores Ltd [1959] AC 20, [1958] 2 WLR
513, [1958] 1 All ER 607   4.2
Bewlay (Tobacconist) Limited v British Bata Shoe Co Limited [1959] 1 WLR
45, [1958] 3 All ER 653, (1959) 103 SJ 33   4.2
Birch (A & W) Ltd v PB (Sloane) Ltd (1956) 106 LJ 204, [1956] JPL 514, 167
EG 283   4.2
Blunden v Frogmore Investments Limited [2002] EWCA Civ 573   2.7
Blythwood Plant Hire Ltd v Spiers Ltd (in receivership) [1992] 2 EGLR 103,
[1992] 48 EG 117   5.6, 8.4

Boots The Chemists Ltd v Pinkland Ltd [1992] 28 EG 118   5.6, 5.9, 8.4

Bristol Cars Ltd v RKH (Hotels) Ltd (in liquidation) (1979) 38 P & CR 411,
(1979) 251 EG 1279, CA   3.5

CBS United Kingdom Ltd v London Scottish Properties Ltd (1985) 2 EGLR
125, (1985) 275 EG 718   5.3

Cairnplace Ltd v CBL (Property Investment) Company Ltd [1984] 1 WLR 696,
[1984] 1 All ER 315, (1984) 128 SJ 281, CA   5.4, 5.10

Cardogan v McCarthy & Stone Developments Ltd [1996] NPC 77, [1996]
EGCS 94, (1996) *The Independent*, 17 June, CA   4.2

Cardshops v John Lewis Properties [1983] QB 161, [1982] 3 WLR 803, [1982]
3 All ER 746, (1982) 263 EG 791   10.2

Carradine Properties Ltd v Aslam [1976] 1 WLR 442, [1976] 1 All ER 573,
(1975) 32 P & CR 12   2.6

Chabba v Turbogame Limited [2001] EWCA Civ 1073   6.4

Charles Follett Ltd v Cabtell Investment Co Ltd (1987) 283 EG 195, (1988) 55
P & CR 36, [1986] 2 EGLR 76, CA   8.4

Chez Gerard Ltd v Greene Ltd (1983) 268 EG 575   4.3

City of London Corporation v Fell; Herbert Duncan Ltd v Cluttons [1993] QB
589, [1993] 2 WLR 710, [1993] 2 All ER 449, [1993] 4 EG 115   8.9

Commercial Union Life Assurance v Moustafa [1999] 2 EGLR 44, [1999] 24
EG 155, [1999] L & TR 489, QBD   2.7

Conway v Arthur [1988] 2 EGLR 113, [1988] 40 EG 120   8.4

Co-operative Insurance Society Limited v Argyll Stores (Holding) Limited
[1998] AC 1, [1997] 2 WLR 898, [1997] 3 All ER 297, [1997] 23 EG 141   5.9

Co-operative Wholesale Society Limited v National Westminster Bank plc;
Broadgate Square v Lehman Bros; Scottish Amicable Life Assurance Society
v Middleton Potts & Co; Prudential Nominees v Greenham Trading [1995]
01 EG 111, [1994] EGCS 184, [1994] NPC 147, CA   5.9

Crowhurst Park, Re [1974] 1 All ER 991, [1974] 1 WLR 583, (1973) 118 SJ 331   4.3

Davy's of London (Wine Merchants) Limited v The City of London and Saxon
Land BV [2004] EWHC 2224   5.3

Department of the Enviroment v Allied Freehold Property Trust Ltd [1992] 45
EG 156, Cty Ct   5.9, 8.4

Department of the Environment v Royal Insurance (1987) 54 P & CR 26,
(1987) 282 EG 208, [1987] 1 EGLR 83   10.2

Dolgellau Golf Club v Hett [1998] 2 EGLR 75, [1998] L & TR 217, (1998) 76 P
& CR 526, CA   4.3

Drummond (Inspector of Taxes) v Austin Brown [1986] Ch 52, [1984] 3 WLR
381, [1984] 2 All ER 699, CA   10.4

Durley House Limited v Cadogan [2000] 1 EGLR 60, [1999] EGCS 120, (1999)
96(43) LSG 34, ChD   5.5

Edicron Ltd v William Whiteley Ltd [1984] 1 WLR 59, [1984] 1 All ER 219,
(1983) 47 P & CR 625, CA   10.2

Edwards v Thompson [1990] 29 EG 41, (1990) 60 P & CR 222, [1990] LS Gaz
   February 21, 33, CA   4.2
Edwards (H) & Sons Limited v Central London Commercial Estates Limited
   [1984] 2 EGLR 103   5.3
Electricity Supply Nominees Ltd v Thorn EMI Retail (1991) Ltd (1991) 63 P &
   CR 143, [1991] 2 EGLR 46, [1991] 35 EG 114   9.3
English Exporters (London) Ltd v Eldonwall Ltd [1973] Ch 415, [1973] 2
   WLR 435, [1973] 1 All ER 726, (1973) 225 EG 433   8.4
Espresso Coffee Machine Co Ltd v Guardian Assurance Co Ltd [1959] 1 WLR
   250, [1959] 1 All ER 458, (1959) 103 SJ 200   4.2
Esselte AB v Pearl Assurance plc [1997] 1 WLR 891, [1997] 2 All ER 41, [1997]
   2 EG 124   1.3, 7.1, 7.6, 10.2

Falcon Pipes v Stanhope (1967) 117 NLJ 1345, (1967) 204 EG 1243   2.6
Fourbuoys plc v Newport Borough Council [1994] 1 EGLR 138, [1994] 24 EG
   156   5.6
Free Grammar School of John Lyon v Mahew [1997] 17 EG 163, (1997) TLR 5   2.6
French v Commercial Union [1993] 24 EG 115   5.5, 8.4, 8.5
Fuller v Judy Properties Ltd [1991] 2 EGLR 41, [1991] 31 EG 63   2.9

Garston v Scottish Widows Fund and Life Assurance Society [1996] 1 WLR 834,
   [1996] 4 All ER 282, [1996] 23 EG 131   3.3
Germax Securities Ltd v Spiegal (1978) P & CR 204, (1978) 123 SJ 164, (1978)
   250 EG 449, CA   2.6
Gilmoor Caterers Limited v St Bartholomew's Hospital Governors [1956] 1 QB
   387, [1956] 2 WLR 419, [1956] 1 All ER 314   4.2
Gregson v Cyril Lord Ltd [1963] 1 WLR 41, [1962] 3 All ER 907, (1963) 106 SJ
   988   4.3
Gwynedd Council v Grunshaw [1999] 4 All ER 304, [1999] NPC 101, (1999)
   149 NLJ 1286, CA   6.3

Hancock & Willis v GMS Syndicate Ltd (1982) 265 EG 473   1.4
Harvey Textiles Limited v Hillel (1979) 249 EG 1063   4.3
Herongrove Limited v Wates City of London Properties plc [1988] 1 EGLR 82,
   (1988) 24 EG 108   2.3
Hodgson v Armstrong [1967] 2 QB 299, [1967]2 WLR 311, [1967] 1 All ER
   307   6.4
Hogarth Health Club v Westbourne Investments Ltd (1989) 59 P & CR 212,
   [1990] 1 EGLR 89, [1990] 02 EG 69, CA   11.2

Janes (Gowns) Ltd v Harlow Development Corporation (1979) 253 EG 799   5.6, 8.4
Joel v Swaddle [1957] 1 WLR 1094, [1957] 3 All ER 325, (1957) 101 SJ 850   4.2
Junction Estates Ltd v Cope (1974) 27 P & CR 482   5.4

Kammin's Ballrooms Co Ltd v Zenith Investments (Torquay) Ltd [1971] AC
   850, [1970] 3 WLR 278, [1970] 2 All ER 871   3.5

Keepers and Governors of the Free Grammar School of John Lyon v Mayhew
(1997) 29 HLR 719, [1997] 1 EGLR 88, [1997] 17 EG 163, CA   3.8

Leathwoods v Total Oil (Great Britain) Limited (1985) 51 P & CR 20, (1984)
270 EG 1083, [1985] 2 EGLR 237   4.2
Lloyds Bank Ltd v City of London Corporation [1983] Ch 192, [1982] 3 WLR
1138, [1983] 1 All ER 92, CA   10.1
London Baggage Co (Charing Cross) Ltd v Railtrack plc (No 2) [2003] 1
EGLR 141   10.6
London Hilton Jewellers Ltd v Hilton International Hotels Ltd [1990] 1 EGLR
112, [1990] 20 EG 74, CA   4.2

Mannai Investment Company Limited v The Eagle Star Life Assurance
Company Limited [1997] AC 749, [1997] 2 WLR 945, [1997] 3 All ER 352,
[1997] 24 EG 122, [1997] 25 EG 138   2.6
Marazzi v Global Grange Limited [2002] EWHC 3010, Ch, [2003] 34 EG 59   4.2
Marks (Morris) v British Waterways Board [1963] 1 WLR 1008, [1963] 3 All ER
28, (1963) 107 SJ 512   4.2
Method Development Limited v Jones [1971] 1 WLR 168, [1971] 1 All ER
1027, (1970) 115 SJ 13   4.3
Meyer v Riddick (1989) 60 P & CR 50, [1990] 1 EGLR 107, [1990] 18 EG 97,
CA   2.10
Mirza v Nicola [1990] 2 EGLR 73, [1990] 30 EG 92, CA   4.2
Morrisons Holdings v Manders Property (Wolverhampton) Ltd [1976] 2 All ER
205, [1976] 1 WLR 533, (1975) 120 SJ 63   10.2
Morrow v Nadeem [1986] 1 WLR 1381, [1987] 1 All ER 237, (1986) 279 EG
1083, CA   2.6
Murphy (J) and Sons Limited v Railtrack plc [2001] EWCA Civ 679, [2002] 1
EGLR 48   5.5

Nasim v Wilson (1975) 119 SJ 611   2.7
National Car Parks Ltd v The Paternoster Consortium Ltd [1990] 15 EG 53,
[1990] 1 EGLR 99   5.3
National Justice Compania Naviera SA v Prudential Assurance [1993] 2 Lloyds
Rep 68, [1993] 37 EG 158, (1993) *The Times*, 5 March   5.5

O'May v City of London Real Property Co Ltd [1983] 2 AC 726, [1982] 2 WLR
407, [1982] 1 All ER 660, HL   5.2, 5.6, 5.8, 5.9

Palisade Investments Ltd v Colln Estates Ltd [1992] 2 EGLR 94, [1992] 27 EG
134, CA   4.2
Pearson v Alyo (1989) 60 P & CR 56, [1990] 1 EGLR 114, [1990] 25 EG 69, CA

                                                                                            2.6
Pennycook v Shaws (EAL) Limited [2003] Ch 399, [2003] 2 WLR 1265, [2003]
EWHC 2769, Ch, [2003] 3 EGLR 28   3.4

Plessey & Co v Eagle Pensions Fund Ltd [1990] 35 EG 52   10.2
Price v Esso Petroleum Co Limited (1980) 255 EG 243   4.2
Price v West London Investment Building Society [1964] 1 WLR 616, [1964] 2
    All ER 318, 108 SJ 276, CA   2.7

R v Gravesend County Council ex parte Patchett [1993] 2 EGLR 125, [1993]
    26 EG 125, [1993] COD 12   8.2
Ratners (Jewellers) Limited v Lemnoll (1980) 255 EG 987   8.4
Reohorn v Barry Corporation [1956] 1 WLR 845, [1956] 2 All ER 742, (1956)
    100 SJ 509   4.2
Romulus Trading Co Ltd v Henry Smith's Charity Trustees (1989) 60 P & CR
    62, [1990] 2 EGLR 75, [1990] 32 EG 41, CA   4.2
Rous (Earl of Stradbroke) v Mitchell [1991] 1 WLR 469, [1991] 1 All ER 676,
    (1990) PLB 46, CA   2.6

Sabella Limited v Montgomery; *sub nom* Montgomery v Sabella Ltd [1998] 1
    EGLR 65, [1998] 09 EG 153, (1998) 75 P & CR D41, CA   2.6
Safeway Food Stores v Morris (1980) 254 EG 1091   2.3
Salomon v Akiens (1992) 65 P & CR 364, [1993] 14 EG 97, [1992] EGCS 131,
    CA   3.5
Scholl Manufacturing Co Ltd v Clifton (Slim-Line) Ltd [1967] Ch 41, [1966] 3
    WLR 575, [1966] 3 All ER 16, CA   2.3
Shelley v United Artists Corporation Ltd (1989) 60 P & CR 241, [1990] 1
    EGLR 103, [1990] 16 EG 73   2.8
Sight & Sound Education Ltd v Brooks etc Ltd [1999] 3 EGLR 45, [1999] 43
    EG 161, ChD   10.2
Smith v Draper (1990) 60 P & CR 252, [1990] 2 EGLR 69, [1990] 27 EG 69,
    CA   2.6
Stevens & Cutting Ltd v Anderson [1990] 1 EGLR 95, [1990] 11 EG 70, CA   3.5
Stevenson and Rush (Holdings) Limited v Langdon (1979) 38 P & CR 208,
    (1978) 122 SJ 827, (1978) 249 EG 743, CA   5.10
Stidolph v American School in London Educational Trust (1969) 20 P & CR
    802, (1969) 113 SJ 689, CA   2.6
Stream Properties v Davies [1972] 1 WLR 645, [1972] 2 All ER 746, (1972) 222
    EG 1203   8.1
Stylo Shoes Ltd v Manchester Royal Exchange Ltd (1967) 204 EG 803   5.6
Stylo Shoes Ltd v Price Tailors Ltd [1960] Ch 396, [1960] 2 WLR 8, [1959] 3
    All ER 901   2.7
Sun Life Assurance plc v Thales Tracs Limited and another [2001] 1 WLR
    1562, [2001] 2 EGLR 57, [2001] EWCA Civ 704, , QBD   10.1
Sunrose v Gould [1961] 3 All ER 1142, [1962] 1 WLR 20, (1962) 105 SJ 988,
    CA   2.6

Teesside Indoor Bowls Ltd v Stockton on Tees Borough Council [1990] 2
    EGLR 87, [1990] 46 EG 116   4.3
Tegerdine v Brooks [1978] 1 EGLR 33, (1977) 36 P & CR 261, (1977) 121 SJ
    155, CA   2.6

Thorn EMI Plc v Pinkland Ltd [1992] 28 EG 118   8.4

VCS Car Park Management Limited v Regional Railways North East Limited
    [2001] Ch 1211, [2000] 3 WLR 370, [2000] 1 All ER 403, [2000] 1 EGLR 57   4.3

Walker v Daniels [2000] 1 WLR 1382   6.8
Wallis Fashion Group Limited v CGU Life Assurance Limited [2000] 2 EGLR
    49   5.8
Webber (CA) (Transport) Ltd v Railtrack plc [2004] 1 WLR 32, [2003] EWCA
    1167, CA   2.7
Willis v British Commonwealth Universities' Association [1965] 1 QB 140,
    [1964] 2 WLR 946, [1964] 2 All ER 39, CA   4.3

Yamaha-Kemble Music (UK) Ltd v ARC Properties Ltd [1990] 1 EGLR 261,
    [1989] NPC 5   2.6

Zarvos v Pradhan [2003] EWCA Civ 208, [2003] 26 EG 180   4.3

TABLE OF STATUTES

References are to paragraph numbers and Appendices

Companies Act 1985
  s 287 — 2.7
  s 736 — 2.10
Companies Act 1989 — 2.10
Costs of Leases Act 1958 — 5.10

European Convention on the
  Protection of Human Rights
  and Fundamental Freedoms — 6.8

Human Rights Act 1998 — 6.8, App 1

Land Compensation Act 1973
  Pt 3 — App 1
Land Registration Act 2002
  s 87 — 3.9
Landlord and Tenant Act 1927 — 3.6, 3.7, 11.3, App 2, App 3
  Pt I — 11.1
  s 18 — 9.1
  s 23 — 2.7
    (1) — 2.7
  s 34 — App 3
Landlord and Tenant Act 1954 — 1.1, 1.3, 1.5, 1.6, 2.2, 2.6–2.10, 3.3, 3.5, 3.6, 3.9, 4.3, 5.2–5.5, 5.8, 5.10, 6.8, 10.6, 11.3, 12.1, 12.2, 12.4, 12.5, App 1
  Pt II — 1.1, 5.3, App 2
  s 23 — 1.5
    (1) — 1.4
    (1A) — 1.4, 6.4, 6.5
    (2) — 1.4

s 23(4) — 1.4
ss 24–28 — App 1
s 24 — 2.8, 2.11, 7.6, 8.9, App 1
  (1) — 2.4, 2.5
  (2) — 3.3, 6.5
  (2A) — App 1
  (2B) — App 1
  (2C) — 2.5
ss 24A–24D — App 1
s 24A — 8.1, 8.9
  (1) — 8.6
  (3) — 8.3, 8.4, 8.9
s 24B — 6.6, 8.1, 8.3
s 24C — 8.1, 8.7
  (2) — 3.2, 6.6, 8.7
  (3) — 6.6
  (6) — 8.7
s 24D — 8.1, 8.7
  (3) — 6.6
s 25 — 1.2, 2.1–2.9, 3.1, 3.2, 3.4–3.6, 3.8, 4.2, 4.3, 6.1, 6.4–6.6, 7.1, 7.3, 7.4, 8.1–8.3, 10.2, App 1, App 2, App 3
  (8) — 2.3, App 1
s 26 — 1.2, 2.1, 2.4–2.6, 2.8, 2.9, 3.1–3.3, 3.5, 3.7, 3.8, 4.3, 6.1, 6.4–6.6, 7.3, 7.4, 8.1–8.3, 10.1, 10.2, App 1, App 2, App 3
  (4) — 7.4
  (6) — 3.1, App 1
s 27 — 7.4, 7.5
  (1) — 7.2
  (1A) — 2.4, 7.1
  (2) — 7.4, 7.6
s 29 — 3.5
  (2)–(6) — 2.5
  (2) — 6.4
  (5) — 2.5, 7.7

Landlord and Tenant Act 1954 –
cont

s 29A	2.4, 3.1, App 1
(3)	App 1
s 29B	3.5–3.7, App 1
s 30	3.1
(1)	2.3, 4.1, 10.1, App 1
(a)–(d)	10.1
(e)	10.1, App 1
(f)	4.2, 6.4, 10.1, 12.4, 12.6, App 1
(1)(g)	4.3, 10.1, App 1
(1A)	4.3, App 1
(1B)	4.3, App 1
(2A)	4.3
(3)	4.3
s 31A	4.1, 6.4, 6.5, App 1
(1)	4.2
s 32(1)	5.1
(2)	5.1, 6.4, 6.5
s 34	5.5, 8.4, 8.5, 8.7, App 1
(1)	5.5, 8.7
(2)	5.6, 8.7
(4)	5.2
s 35	5.8, App 1
(2)	5.2, 5.8
s 36	6.11
(2)	5.1, 6.11
s 37	10.1, 10.2, 10.4, 10.5, App 1
(1C)	10.1
(2)	10.2
(3A)	10.2
s 37A(1)	10.5
(2)	10.5
s 38(1)	1.6, 5.10
(2)	10.6
s 38A	1.6, 10.5
s 40	2.2, 2.4, 2.9, 2.12, 3.2, App 1, App 3
(1)	App 1, App 2
(2)	App 1, App 2
(3)	2.12, App 1
(4)	App 1

s 40(5)	2.2, App 1
(8)	App 1
s 40A	2.2
s 40B	2.2, App 1
s 41	6.4, 6.5
(1)	2.10
(2)	2.10
s 41A	2.11
(6)	2.11
s 42	2.10, 6.4, 6.5
(1)	2.10
(2)	1.4
(c)	8.9
(3)	4.3
s 43(3)	1.5
s 44	2.8, App 1
s 46(2)	App 1
s 64	4.2, 5.9
s 66(4)	2.7
s 67	2.12, App 1
s 69(1)	3.3
s 146	2.9, 9.1, 9.4
Sch 6, para 3	2.8
para 6	2.8
para 7	2.8
Landlord and Tenant (Covenants) Act 1995	5.2, 5.8, 8.9
s 17	2.7
Landlord and Tenant (Licensed Premises) Act 1990	1.5
Law of Property Act 1925	2.12
Law of Property Act 1969	8.1
Leasehold Property (Repairs) Act 1938	9.4
Recorded Delivery Service Act 1962	2.7
Rent Act 1977	App 1
Rent (Agriculture) Act 1976	App 1
Telecommunications Act 1984	12.2
Sch 2	12.1

TABLE OF STATUTORY INSTRUMENTS

References are to paragraph numbers and Appendices

County Court Rules 1981, SI 1981/1687
  Ord 43   6.7
       r 2(2)   6.7
Civil Procedure Rules 1998, SI 1998/3132   6.1, 6.4, 6.7, 6.8, 6.12, 8.6
  r 1.4(2)(e)   6.12
  r 3.10   6.3
  r 6.2   6.4
  r 6.3(3)   6.4
  r 6.14   6.4
  Pt 7   6.4
  r 7.5(2)   6.4
  r 7.6(3)   6.4
  Pt 8   6.4–6.6, App 1
  r 8.3   6.5
  r 10   6.5
  Pt 22   6.4
  PD 22, para 3.1   6.4
  Pt 23   6.6
  r 29.3   6.8
  r 30.2   6.3
  r 31.6   6.8
  Pt 35   6.8
  r 35.3   5.5
  r 35.6   6.8
  r 35.7   6.8
  r 35.8   6.8
  r 35.10   6.8
  r 35.12   6.8
  PD35, para 1   6.8
  Pt 36   6.9
  r 38.2   7.7
  Pt 44   6.10
  r 44.3(6)   6.10
  Pt 52   6.11
  PD 52   6.11
  Pt 56   6.1
  r 56.2   6.2, 6.3
  r 56.3   6.4
       (3)(c)   6.7

Civil Procedure Rules 1998, SI 1998/3132 – *cont*

PD 56	6.1
PD 56, para 2.2	6.2
para 2.3	6.2
para 2.4	6.2
para 2.5	6.2
para 3.4	6.4
para 3.5	6.4
para 3.7	6.4
para 3.9	6.4
para 3.10	6.5
para 3.11	6.5
para 3.12	6.5
para 3.13	6.5
para 3.17	6.6
para 3.18	6.6
para 3.19	6.6
Sch 2	6.7

Landlord and Tenant Act 1954 (Appropriate Multiplier) Order 1990, SI 1990/363 — 10.2

Landlord and Tenant Act 1954 Part 2 (Notices) Regulations 2004, SI 2004/1005 — 2.3
Sch 2 — App 1

Regulatory Reform (Business Tenancies) (England and Wales) Order 2003, SI 2003/3096 — 1.1, 1.2, 1.4, 1.6, 2.1, 2.2, 2.5, 2.10, 3.2, 3.5, 4.3, 7.1, 7.6, 8.1, 10.2, App 1

Rules of the Supreme Court 1965, SI 1965/1776 — 6.8

Chapter 1

THE STATUTORY TENANCY UNDER THE LANDLORD AND TENANT ACT 1954, PART II

1.1 DEFINITIONS

Security of tenure is conferred on business tenants by the Landlord and Tenant Act 1954, Part II as amended by the Regulatory Reform (Business Tenancies) (England and Wales) Order 2003 (referred to in this book as 'the RRO'). Accordingly, references in this book to 'the Act' are to that statute as so amended, unless otherwise stated.

1.2 TRANSITIONAL PROVISIONS

The RRO came into force on 1 June 2004. However, it has no effect in cases where before that date the landlord had given a Section 25 Notice or the tenant had made a Section 26 Request.

It follows that the 'old law' and the 'new law' are running in parallel, and will continue to do so probably for several years:

–   where the Section 25 Notice was given or the Section 26 Request was made on or before 31 May 2004, the old law applies and will continue to apply;

–   where the Section 25 Notice was given or the Section 26 Request was made on or after 1 June 2004, the new law applies.

1.3 THE PROTECTION IN OUTLINE

A business tenancy will not come to an end on the expiration of a fixed term; nor can a landlord terminate a periodic tenancy by serving notice to quit. So long as the tenant remains in occupation, the tenancy will continue effectively on the same terms and at the same rent until it is determined in one of the ways specified by the Act (*Esselte AB v Pearl Assurance plc* [1997] 2 EG 124).

Upon the expiry of the business tenancy, the tenant may apply to the court for a new tenancy and the landlord may only object to that application on grounds stipulated by the Act. Any new tenancy will also be protected by the Act.

1.4 WHAT IS A BUSINESS TENANCY?

In order to qualify for protection, the tenancy must be a business tenancy. There are a number of requirements which must be satisfied.

(1) There must be a tenancy (s 23(1) of the Act). This includes an agreement for lease and an underlease. A licence is not protected.

(2) Premises must be wholly or partly occupied for business purposes by the tenant or his employees or by an associated company of a corporate tenant (ss 23(1) and 42(2)). If the tenant is an individual and the premises are occupied by a company owned and/or controlled by that individual, the tenant's tenancy was not protected under the old law, but has been within the Act since 1 June 2004 (s 23(1A) inserted by the RRO). Occupation need not be continuous, provided that the 'thread of continuity' of business user is not broken (*Hancock & Willis v GMS Syndicate Ltd* (1982) 265 EG 473).

(3) Business includes trade, profession or employment (s 23(2)).

(4) The lease must not prohibit business use altogether (s 23(4)).

1.5 EXCLUSIONS FROM THE ACT

In addition to those tenancies that fail to satisfy the requirements of s 23, certain specified tenancies are excluded from the protection of the Act. They include the following:

(1) tenancies at will;

(2) agricultural holdings (which are subject to protection provided by a separate legislative system) and farm business tenancies;

(3) mining leases;

(4) service tenancies, for example where the holder of an employment position occupies premises as a condition of such employment and the occupation continues only for the duration of the employment, the exclusion will apply provided that the tenancy is in writing and states the purpose for which it is granted;

(5) tenancies for 6 months or less unless there is a provision in the lease to renew or extend the tenancy for more than 6 months or the tenant (or a predecessor in the same business) has occupied the premises for more than 12 months (s 43(3)).

Tenancies of premises with licences for the sale of intoxicating liquor (ie pubs) were once excluded but were brought within the Act by the Landlord and Tenant (Licensed Premises) Act 1990.

1.6 CONTRACTING OUT

As a general rule, the Act prohibits contracting out of the protection of the Act (s 38(1)). However, a prospective landlord and tenant may agree that a tenancy, yet to be created, should be excluded from the Act. Under the old law, it was necessary to obtain an order from the county court before the lease was completed. That requirement was abolished and replaced by the RRO which inserted a new s 38A into the Act. Since 1 June 2004, the procedure for contracting out has been:

(1) the prospective landlord must serve on the prospective tenant a notice in, or substantially in, a prescribed form;

(2) if the tenant becomes contractually bound (ie the earlier of exchange or completion takes place) more than 2 weeks after service of the notice, the tenant must acknowledge the notice in a prescribed form;

(3) if the tenant is to become contractually bound within 2 weeks of the notice, the tenant must swear a statutory declaration in a prescribed form; and

(4) the lease must state that the appropriate formalities have been complied with.

Section 38A also renders void any agreement to surrender a business lease in the future unless a similar procedure is followed.

Chapter 2

THE LANDLORD'S POSITION

2.1 INITIAL CONSIDERATIONS

A landlord who has an opportunity to bring a business tenancy to an end must first consider whether he wishes to, and legitimately can, object to a new tenancy being granted and whether the market rent is higher or lower than the existing contractual rent.

A landlord who wishes to, and legitimately can, object to a new tenancy being granted will normally wish to bring the existing tenancy to an end as soon as the lease would otherwise have expired (but see **2.4** for possible exceptions).

A landlord who would be happy to grant a new business tenancy and is confident that the current market rent is higher than the existing contractual rent will also wish to bring the existing tenancy to an end as soon as the lease would otherwise have expired, so that a new lease at a market rent can begin as soon as possible.

Where the passing rent under the existing tenancy is higher than the current market rent, a landlord's first thought may well be to maintain the current tenancy for as long as possible in the hope that the tenant will not take prompt steps to terminate it. This would have been effective to keep the higher rent payable under the old law, though the tenant may always thwart the strategy by serving a Section 26 Request (see **3.2**). It is now much less likely to be effective, because of changes made by the RRO to interim rent procedures. Under the new law, where a Section 25 Notice is served (or a Section 26 Request made) on or after 1 June 2004, either the landlord or the tenant can apply for interim rent, and that interim rent will be payable from the earliest date which could have been specified in the Section 25 Notice or in the Section 26 Request, as the case may be. (In practice, of course, the passing rent would remain payable unless and until the interim rent was agreed or determined, but that interim rent would have retrospective effect from the end of the contractual term, giving the tenant a right to a refund, unless the parties agreed otherwise).

For more comments about interim rent, see Chapter 8.

Whatever the landlord's view, action must be planned and decisions taken well in advance.

2.2   SECTION 40 NOTICE

Obtaining information

A Section 40 Notice is served by the landlord on the tenant and requires the tenant to say whether he occupies premises for business purposes and whether any sub-tenancies are in existence. The importance of this is that, if a Section 25 Notice is served on the immediate tenant, the landlord will become the competent landlord for the purposes of the Act in respect of the sub-tenants and have the power to serve Section 25 Notices on the sub-tenants (see **2.8**). However, the tenant need neither state whether any sub-tenant is carrying on a business nor reveal any terms of the sub-lease.

A Section 40 Notice must be in a prescribed form. A copy of the current form is included in Appendix 1.

The Act requires a tenant to reply to a Section 40 Notice within 1 month of service.

Under the old law there was no statutory sanction for failing to give answers but it was believed (and previous editions of this book said) that if the landlord suffered any financial loss, he 'may well have a claim' for breach of statutory duty.

Since 1 June 2004, there is a statement in the Act that any breach of a duty imposed by s 40 may be made the subject of civil proceedings for breach of statutory duty, in which a court may order compliance and may make an award of damages (s 40B inserted by the RRO).

Also since 1 June 2004, a tenant who receives a Section 40 Notice and replies to it has an additional duty to correct any incorrect information given. That duty arises if the tenant becomes aware that information given is not, or is no longer, correct within a period of 6 months beginning with the date of service of the Section 40 Notice. The corrected information must be given within one month of the date on which the tenant becomes aware (s 40(5)). If the tenant transfers his interest and gives the landlord written notice of the fact of the transfer and the name and address of the transferee (which the lease will almost always require to be done anyway), on giving that notice, the tenant ceases to be under any duty imposed by s 40, which obviously includes the duty to correct incorrect information (s 40A inserted by the RRO).

2.3 SECTION 25 NOTICE

Time-limits: diary dates

Section 25 Notices:

–   may be served at any time not earlier than 12 months before the expiry date – diarise 364 days before expiry date for earliest service;

–   must give at least 6 months' notice of termination – diarise 6 months plus one week before expiry date;

–   diarise 2 weeks before the termination date to check whether an interim rent application has been made, and make one if necessary (see Chapter 8).

Form of Notice

Section 25 Notices must be in the appropriate form prescribed by statutory instrument (Landlord and Tenant Act 1954 Part 2 (Notices) Regulations 2004) which advises the tenant of his rights or in a form 'substantially to the like effect' (see **2.6**). Under the old law, there was only one prescribed form of Section 25 Notice. Since 1 June 2004, there have been two main versions of the prescribed form:

(1) Form 1, to be used if the landlord is willing to grant a new tenancy. A copy of this is included in Appendix 1.

(2) Form 2, to be used if the landlord wishes to oppose the grant of a new tenancy. A copy of this is also included in Appendix 1.

The date specified for termination must be no earlier than the lease could end under common law, that is, the end of a fixed term or expiry of a notice to quit to end a periodic tenancy.

The specified termination date must be not less than 6 nor more than 12 months from the date of service of the notice.

The notice must specify in full the premises to which the notice relates. A small error in this will not invalidate the notice: for example omitting reference to a garage (*Safeway Food Stores v Morris* (1980) 254 EG 1091). Omitting reference to basement car parking in a lease of two office storeys did invalidate a notice (*Herongrove Limited v Wates City of London Properties plc* (1988) 24 EG 108). The best practice therefore is to quote the definition in the lease and then follow it by a specific reference to the lease, eg 'being the premises demised by a lease dated (   ) and made between (   )'.

If the Landlord is not opposed to the grant of a new tenancy, the notice must contain the landlord's proposals as to:

(1) the property to be comprised in the new tenancy;

(2) the rent to be payable under the new tenancy;

(3) the other terms of the new tenancy (s 25(8)).

This is a radical change from the old law, under which the landlord did not have to set out his proposals until he responded to the tenant's court application for a new tenancy, since the tenant could not make such an application until 2 months had passed.

A notice which states that the landlord is opposed to the grant of a new tenancy must specify the ground(s) of objection by reference to the relevant subsection(s) of s 30(1). These are unchanged and are set out in Chapter 4.

Under the old law, the tenant had to notify the landlord within 2 months of service of the notice whether or not he was prepared to give up possession. If he wished to apply for a new tenancy, he had to do so no earlier than 2 months and no later than 4 months after service of the notice.

Under the new law, all this has changed. The tenant no longer has to serve a counter notice at all, and can apply to the court for a new tenancy at any time up to and including the termination date specified in the landlord's Section 25 Notice.

Practical points on choice of termination date

If there is a lease which has not expired, check carefully when it comes to an end and pay attention to the expression 'term of years from' which usually means 'from but excluding'. If in doubt, add an extra day.

Having decided the last day of the lease, remember there is no requirement that a Section 25 Notice shall terminate the tenancy on that date. Termination cannot be earlier, but can be (and often is) later.

It is common to see a break clause contained in a lease in the landlord's favour, eg a 6-month redevelopment clause providing that if the landlord wants to redevelop he can serve contractual notice. By serving a break notice the landlord can determine the lease but not the tenancy. He also has to serve a Section 25 Notice, which in this example will object to a new tenancy on ground (f). If the tenant successfully defeats the Section 25 Notice, then the contractual notice necessarily fails too. Where there is a periodic tenancy or a break clause, a Section 25 Notice can double as a contractual or common law notice (*Scholl Manufacturing Co Ltd v Clifton (Slim-Line) Ltd* [1967] Ch 41), but if a Section 25 Notice is used to serve a dual purpose and for some reason it does not comply with the requirements of the lease, there will be no contractual notice and consequently no effective Section 25 Notice.

2.4 TIMING AND TACTICS

The landlord must decide what he wants to do with the premises and whether he wishes to object to a new tenancy well in advance of the expiry date of the lease and preferably at least a year ahead. The tenant can serve a Section 26 Request for a new tenancy at any time later than one year before the expiry date.

A Section 25 Notice terminating a tenancy can be served by the landlord at any time later than 12 months before the tenancy expires. A Section 40 Notice can be served by a landlord at any time later than 2 years before the tenancy expires.

The well-organised landlord will serve his Section 40 Notice, say, 15 months before expiry, check the result against his management records, serve Section 40 Notices on sub-tenants, and serve his Section 25 Notice(s) 11 months and 3 weeks before expiry.

That well-organised landlord must remember that if he is not objecting to renewal he will have to set out his proposals for the property to be comprised in the new tenancy, the new rent and the other terms of the new tenancy in his Section 25 Notice. If he is objecting to renewal, he will have to remember that the tenant could apply to the court for a new tenancy the very next day, and move swiftly towards forcing the landlord to disclose the evidence which he proposes to use to support his objection.

The poorly advised or disorganised landlord who does not achieve this has to remember that so long as no Section 25 Notice has been served his tenant may serve a Section 26 Request for a new tenancy at any time later than 12 months before expiry, extending the expiry date and the period during which the old rent is paid to a date up to 12 months from the date of the Section 26 Request. It is essential therefore to serve one's notice before the other party does so.

EXAMPLE

Lease will expire on 25 December 2005.

Landlord could serve Section 25 Notice after 26 December 2004 terminating the tenancy on 25 December 2005. But if the landlord has not served a Section 25 Notice earlier the tenant could serve a Section 26 Request on 26 June 2005 extending the tenancy to 24 June 2006, and the new rent would not start until then.

In a case like this, a Section 40 Notice served by a landlord will show a clear intention that the landlord intends to serve a Section 25 Notice and may enable the tenant to get in first. The usual procedure is for the landlord to serve a Section 25 Notice based on the information in his own records and a Section 40 Notice at the same time.

There are two cases where a landlord may deliberately delay:

(1) where the landlord is objecting to a new tenancy under ground (g) (intention to occupy himself), he will fail if he became the landlord by purchase less than 5 years before the specified termination date;

(2) where the landlord is objecting to a new tenancy under ground (f) (intended redevelopment), he will have to prove that he has a settled intention and the ability to redevelop at the date of the court hearing (the later the notice, the later the procedure will start and the more time the landlord will have to obtain planning consent and funding; however, it should be noted that the tenant must be notified when an application is made for planning permission and he then may serve a Section 26 Request specifying the earliest possible termination date and do all he can to accelerate the procedure).

In these cases the landlord will avoid serving a Section 40 Notice in the hope that the tenant will not realise the landlord's need for delay. Note, however, that if the tenant wants to leave and does leave before the end of the contractual term the tenancy will end at the end of the contractual term (s 27(1A)).

Under the new law, either the landlord or the tenant can apply to the court for the grant of a new tenancy (s 24(1)) and the application can be made as soon as the Section 25 Notice has been served or the Section 26 Request made (s 29A). In other words, a landlord wishing to press ahead can start the court proceedings itself and can do so immediately.

2.5   NEW OPTIONS FOR LANDLORDS: ORDER FOR TERMINATION OR APPLY ITSELF FOR NEW LEASE

Under the old law, a landlord objecting to renewal, however strong his grounds for doing so, was faced with the fact that the tenant could not apply for a new tenancy less than 2 months after the date of service of the Section 25 Notice, and might wait to apply for as long as 4 months after the date of service. Only when the tenant had made his court application could the landlord set about proving his case.

Under the new law, a landlord, which has served a Section 25 Notice opposing the grant of a new tenancy, may itself apply to the court for an order for the termination of the tenancy without the grant of a new tenancy. This can be done as early as the day after the Section 25 Notice is served.

Obviously, this allows such a landlord to start the ball rolling much earlier than was possible under the old law.

Note that such an application cannot be made if the landlord or the tenant has already applied to the court for a new tenancy. Note also that a landlord's application for an order for the termination of the existing tenancy without the grant of a new tenancy may not be withdrawn without the consent of the tenant.

(These provisions are in s 29(2)–(6) inclusive.)

Under the old law, only the tenant could apply to the court for a new tenancy.

Under the new law, the landlord which has served a Section 25 Notice not objecting to the grant of a new tenancy can start the ball rolling by applying to the court itself. This can be done as early as the day after the Section 25 Notice of Section 26 Request is served (s 24(1) as amended by the RRO).

This does not allow the landlord to force the tenant to take a new tenancy; the court must dismiss the landlord's application if the tenant tells the court that he does not want a new tenancy (s 29(5)).

Note that such a landlord's application may not be withdrawn without the consent of the tenant (s 24(2C)).

2.6 SOME CASES ON VALIDITY

As stated above, a landlord's Section 25 Notice has to be in a prescribed form or in a form 'substantially to the like effect'. All the decided cases were decided under the old law, but there is no reason to believe they would have been decided differently under the new law.

Whether a Section 25 Notice which is not in the prescribed form passes this test, and is valid, depends not on the number or amount of differences but their importance. What is important is that the recipient tenant must be made aware of its rights and obligations; differences between the form actually used and the prescribed form can only be disregarded where the information actually given to the recipient tenant about its rights and obligations under the Act is in substance as effective as that set out in the prescribed form. It is irrelevant whether the recipient tenant has actually been misled. These guidelines were set out by the Court of Appeal in *Sabella Limited v Montgomery* [1998] 1 EGLR 65, where the material differences, which prevented the form actually used being valid, included the omission of the words which appeared in capitals and surrounded by a box near the top of the prescribed form advising the tenant to 'act quickly' and (where the landlord was objecting to renewal on grounds (b) and (f)) the omission of notes 4(f) and (g) and of paragraph 5 of the notes, which reminded the tenant of its rights to compensation if the landlord obtains possession solely on one or more of grounds (e), (f) and (g).

Contrast the earlier case of *Tegerdine v Brooks* [1978] 1 EGLR 33, where the Court of Appeal held that the omission of a note which related to a notice where the landlord opposed the grant of a new tenancy, which the landlord in this case had not, and a note which related to uncertainties as to who was the landlord, which is also not relevant in this case, were both irrelevant and did not invalidate the Notice which had been given.

If the prescribed form is used, but is completed incorrectly, there is still some scope to overcome the defect.

Errors which have been overcome include an undated notice (*Falcon Pipes v Stanhope* (1967) 117 NLJ 1345), an unsigned notice with a covering letter saying it was served on behalf of the landlord (*Stidolph v American School* (1969) 20 P & CR 802), a notice with a date of termination of 15 July in an unspecified year (*Sunrose v Gould* [1961] 3 All ER 1142) and a notice which gave a termination date 2 years or 1 year early (respectively *Carradine Properties Ltd v Aslam* [1976] 1 WLR 442 and *Germax Securities Ltd v Spiegal* (1978) P & CR 204).

Some errors cannot be overcome, eg misstating the landlord's name (*Yamaha-Kemble Music (UK) Ltd v ARC Properties Ltd* [1990] 1 EGLR 261) or failing to name all the individuals who together made up the landlord (*Pearson v Alyo* [1990] 25 EG 69 and *Smith v Draper*, see below). However, it was said in *Morrow v Nadeem* ((1986) 279 EG 1083) that a mere misdescription of the landlord would not invalidate the notice if the tenant was not misled.

It is possible, following the decision of the House of Lords in *Mannai Investment Company Limited v The Eagle Star Life Assurance Company Limited* [1997] 24 EG 122 and 25 EG 138, that a notice specifying an invalid date of termination would be treated as valid, if it could be said that the tenant who received it could not have been misled as to the intended date. The most likely (or least unlikely) situation in which such a notice might be upheld would be where the landlord is seen to have made an error in calculating the termination date of the contractual term. For example, a lease for 25 years from 25 March 1981 would normally end on 25 March 2006, not 24 March 2006 (assuming there was no evidence that the parties intended the earlier date); if a Section 25 Notice was served specifying a termination date of 24 March 2006 it is tempting to argue that the tenant must have realised that the landlord intended to specify the following day and could not be prejudiced if the notice was upheld on that basis. The argument to the contrary is that *Mannai* was not a case about statutory time-limits under the Act but about a date specified in a break notice governed only by the terms of the relevant lease and common law rules.

Where an apparently invalid Section 25 Notice and an apparently valid Section 25 Notice are served together, it is likely that neither will be treated as valid because the inconsistency between them would confuse the tenant. This follows the Court of Appeal's decision in *Barclays Bank plc v Bee* [2001] EWCA Civ 1126; [2001] 3 EGLR 41, in which the landlord's solicitors served, under cover of the same letter, a Section 25 Notice stating that the landlord would object to the grant of a new tenancy but not indicating on which of the statutory grounds (which, the parties accepted, meant the Notice could not be valid) and another Section 25 Notice stating that the landlord would not oppose an application for a new tenancy. Having considered the possible application of *Mannai*, the Court of Appeal held that a reasonable recipient of the two notices would not have been able to conclude that the apparently invalid notice should be ignored. They would have found the situation confusing and uncertain. In that case, the landlord had gone on to serve another (a third!) Notice, objecting to renewal on grounds (f) and (g) which was held to be the only valid notice served.

If the tenant served a counter notice and then issued proceedings for a new tenancy without challenging the Section 25 Notice as being defective, he may have been estopped from challenging the notice later (as happened in *Free Grammar School of John Lyon v Mayhew* [1997] 17 EG 163). Now that counter notices are not required, it must be likely that issuing proceedings for a new tenancy would create such an estoppel.

It is important to note the following.

(1) There is no provision in the Act allowing a Section 25 Notice to be withdrawn or amended (there seem to be no cases on these points) apart from the special case of a change of competent landlord (see **2.8**), but if a Section 25 Notice is invalid it can be replaced so long as the tenant has not served a Section 26 Request first: *Smith v Draper* [1990] 27 EG 69, where the landlord served a Section 25 Notice which incorrectly named the landlords by omitting some of them. In that case the tenant notified the landlord of his unwillingness to give up possession, but the landlord then served a second correct notice to which the tenant did not respond in time. The Court of Appeal held the second notice was valid and operative and confirmed an order for possession. Such a second notice could obviously include grounds of objection not mentioned in the invalid notice.

(2) A landlord is not limited to a single ground of opposition. He can always abandon a ground of opposition but he cannot amend the Section 25 Notice to add new grounds at a later date. However, beware the implications of *Rous (Earl of Stradbroke) v Mitchell* (1990 PLB 46), a case on agricultural tenancies, where a landlord objected to renewal on a ground which was not true. It was held that because the landlord had recklessly failed to consider whether the ground was true, the notice was fraudulent and therefore invalid. Beware also the danger that a tenant may be prepared to leave, possibly in order to obtain open market concessions in other premises nearby, and all too willing to accept any statutory compensation which is available (see Chapter 10).

(3) As soon as the validity of a notice is challenged by a tenant for reasons which can be identified, a second notice should be served, correcting the error(s), stated to be without prejudice to the validity of the first notice.

2.7   METHODS OF SERVICE

A notice under the Act may be served by personal service, or by leaving it at the addressee's last known place of business in England and Wales (which includes his business address: *Price v West London Investment Building Society* [1964] 1 WLR 616), or sending it there by registered or recorded delivery post. These methods are authorised by s 23 of the Landlord and Tenant Act 1927 which is incorporated into the Act by s 66(4) (s 23 refers to registered post; the Recorded Delivery Service Act 1962 states that a document authorised to be sent by registered post may also be sent by recorded delivery).

A notice to a landlord may be served on his duly authorised agent. Nevertheless, the tenant will not normally have evidence of that authority, so should not use such a method of service if there are alternatives.

There is authority that a notice to a tenant may be served on his solicitors (*Nasim v Wilson* (1975) 119 SJ 611), but the landlord should not rely on this. This does not apply to a counter notice.

A notice to be served on a company may be served on its registered office: Companies Act 1985, s 287.

In practice, the landlord should serve the tenant at the premises and at the address(es) stated in the lease, or in a subsequent licence, or to which rent demands are sent, by recorded delivery. Where the tenant is a company, it should also be served by recorded delivery at its registered office. It may be best to avoid sending out recorded delivery communications on Fridays in case the premises in question are closed on Saturdays and the envelope is returned undelivered for that reason alone.

Where, as here, s 23 of the Landlord and Tenant Act 1927 applies, a notice which is sent by recorded delivery will be deemed to have been served so long as the sender can prove that it was duly posted by recorded delivery (by producing the certificate of posting), even if the intended recipient never receives it: *Commercial Union Life Assurance v Moustafa* [1999] 2 EGLR 44 (a case about a notice served under s 17 of the Landlord and Tenant (Covenants) Act 1995, to which s 23 of the Landlord and Tenant Act 1927 also applies; the notice in question had been posted by recorded delivery and returned by Royal Mail as undelivered and not called for, but nevertheless was held to have been validly served) and *Blunden v Frogmore Investments Limited* [2002] EWCA Civ 573 (where a Section 25 Notice sent by recorded delivery was returned to the landlord's solicitor undelivered, but held to have been validly served).

Section 23(1) of the Landlord and Tenant Act 1927 also deems notices sent by registered post (and therefore, by the Recorded Delivery Service Act 1962, notices sent by recorded delivery) to be served on the date of posting.

For two painful examples see:

Beanby Estates Limited v Egg Stores (Stamford Hill) Limited [2003] EWHC 1252 (Ch)

–   section 25 Notice sent by recorded delivery on 7 January 2002

–   received 9 January 2002

–   tenant applied to the County Court for a new tenancy on 8 May 2002 (more than four months after posting but less than four months after receipt)

–   tenant was out of time.

CA Webber (Transport) Ltd v Railtrack plc [2003] EWCA 1167

–   section 25 Notice sent by recorded delivery on 20 July 2001, specifying a termination date of 22 January 2002

–   not delivered the following day (a Saturday), received on 23 or 24 July 2001

–   tenant argued Section 25 Notice was invalid because the termination date was less than six months after the date of service

–   Court of Appeal disagreed.

If the notice is in fact received by the party to whom it is given, it will have been validly served (*Stylo Shoes Ltd v Price Tailors Ltd* [1960] Ch 396).

2.8   THE COMPETENT LANDLORD

A Section 25 Notice may only be served by the 'competent landlord'. The competent landlord for the purposes of the Act is not necessarily the immediate landlord of the tenant.

The competent landlord is defined by s 44 of the Act as the first person up the chain with an interest of not less than 14 months unexpired. Note, however, that a landlord who has a reversionary interest of less than 14 months unexpired, but is himself a business tenant whose tenancy has not been determined under the Act, will be treated as the competent landlord until a Section 25 Notice is served on him, or he serves a Section 26 Request, because his tenancy will continue automatically until the date specified in such a notice or request (s 24 of the Act).

It goes without saying that this will only arise when the intermediate tenant has sub-let part of his demise to a business occupier (eg a shop with offices above where a retailer has a lease of the whole and has sub-let the offices). If the sub-letting is of the whole for the whole of the term of the head lease, less a few days, the intermediate tenant will not have the protection of the Act, and by the time the superior landlord is able to serve a Section 25 Notice, the head lease will have less than 14 months unexpired.

Figure 1: Who is the competent landlord?

(A)

Tenant has no renewal rights.

Landlord is 'competent landlord' of sub-tenant.

(B)

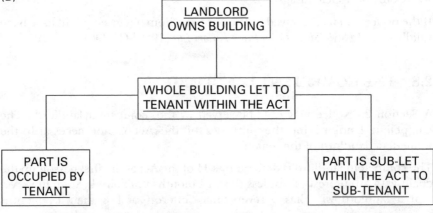

(i) Tenant has renewal rights.

Unless and until the landlord serves Section 25 Notice on tenant <u>or</u> tenant serves Section 26 Request on landlord, tenant is 'competent landlord' of sub-tenant.

However, as soon as one of these hapens, landlord becomes 'competent landlord' of sub-tenant.

(ii) Tenant can only require landlord to grant him a lease of the part occupied by the tenant.

However, landlord can insist that the court orders tenant to take a new lease of the whole building. Tenant's only alternative is not to renew at all.

An intermediate tenant who serves a Section 26 Request on his landlord will by that action cease to be the competent landlord of his tenants. If the intermediate tenant serves a valid and effective Section 25 Notice upon his sub-tenants, then serves a Section 26 Request upon his landlord, the sub-tenants must serve their counter notices on, and make their court application against, the superior landlord. However, what if the sub-tenants do not know about the Section 26 Request and the change of identity of the competent landlord?

Shelley v United Artists Corporation Ltd (1990) 16 EG 73 was such a situation. It was held that the Section 25 Notice was a representation that the intermediate tenant was the competent landlord, which became a misrepresentation when the Section 26 Request was served; and the intermediate tenant had a duty to correct that misrepresentation. A new 25-year lease had been granted to an associated company of the intermediate tenant represented by the same solicitors as the intermediate tenant; the Court of Appeal held that if the new lease had been granted to the original intermediate tenant, it would have been estopped from denying that it was the competent landlord, and the associated company could be in no better position.

Where the misrepresenting intermediate tenant does not obtain a new lease itself, there would seem only to be a claim for damages.

A superior landlord who is a competent landlord is not obliged to obtain the consent of an intermediate landlord before serving a Section 25 Notice on the sub-tenant (Sch 6, para 3).

An intermediate business tenant who has less than 16 months of his lease remaining must notify his immediate landlord of any Section 25 Notices served by him on the sub-tenants or of any Section 26 Request received (Sch 6, para 7).

The superior landlord who becomes a competent landlord (by serving a Section 25 Notice on the immediate tenant, or as a result of the immediate tenant serving a Section 26 Request) has a period of 2 months after the giving of a Section 25 Notice by the intermediate landlord to withdraw it (Sch 6, para 6) and can then serve his own. It follows that a new competent landlord can object to renewal when the former competent landlord did not, or object on other grounds.

In a chain of tenancies, each intermediate tenant must notify his landlord in turn.

It seems from the drafting of the Act that only the competent landlord (or, where the new law applies, the occupying tenant) can apply for interim rent, though there are no cases directly on this point (see Chapter 8). This leaves the intermediate tenant exposed if the superior landlord acts first, because the intermediate tenant can be required to pay an interim rent, but may only recover the old rent from the part(s) sub-let (unless, under the new law, the occupying tenant saves the day by applying itself). This can be solved if the intermediate tenant serves a Section 25 Notice as early as possible and applies for interim rent immediately thereafter, before the superior landlord has time to react to the copy of the notice he receives.

2.9   CONSEQUENCES OF UNLAWFUL ASSIGNMENT

The Act does not define 'tenant', so it presumably means the tenant for the time being. On this basis, where there has been an unlawful assignment, the tenant who is to be served is the assignee – by analogy with Section 146 Notices which must be served on the assignee (*Fuller v Judy Properties Ltd* [1991] 31 EG 63).

If a Section 40 Notice has been served and the reply discloses the unlawful assignment, or if the landlord is aware of the unlawful assignment by other means, and the landlord wishes to reserve his rights to forfeit the lease, a Section 146 Notice should be served followed by a Section 25 Notice specifically without prejudice to the Section 146 Notice (note *Baglarbasi v Deedmethod Ltd* [1991] 29 EG 137 which held that a Section 25 Notice could be served after forfeiture proceedings had been issued).

If there has been an unlawful assignment of which the landlord has not been notified and of which the landlord is not aware, and the landlord therefore serves an invalid Section 25 Notice, the assignee could, if timing allowed, serve a Section 26 Request with the latest possible termination date, but:

–   any financial gain to the assignee would simply increase the landlord's damages claim for breach of covenant against the assignor; and

–   such action would antagonise the landlord at a time when the tenant/ assignee would normally wish the landlord to co-operate by overlooking the breach.

2.10   GROUP OCCUPATION AND TRUSTEE PROVISIONS

By s 42 of the Act, where the tenant is a member of a group of companies and the premises are occupied for business purposes by another member of the group this is treated as occupation by the tenant, who therefore will have security of tenure and renewal rights.

Two companies are members of a group for the purposes of the Act if one is a subsidiary of the other or if both are subsidiaries of a third company. The definition of subsidiary is taken from s 736 of the Companies Act 1985 in the form substituted by the Companies Act 1989, which refers to voting rights and the right to appoint or remove a majority of its board of directors. For practical purposes, if two chains can be established in which more than 50% of the shares in each company is owned by its parent until a common parent is reached and all the shares in each company have equal voting rights, those companies will be in a group. (See Figure 2 below.)

Figure 2: Group companies

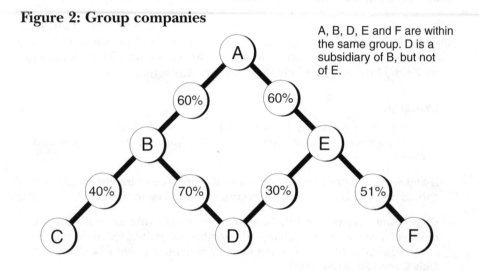

A, B, D, E and F are within the same group. D is a subsidiary of B, but not of E.

The RRO amended s 42(1) to add a third way. Two companies shall be taken as members of a group if the same person has a controlling interest in them both.

Taking the example illustrated above, if A had been an individual and not a company, then under the old law B and E would not have been members of the same group of companies. Under the new law, they are members of the same group of companies.

By s 41(1) of the Act, where a tenancy is held on trust and the premises are occupied for business purposes by beneficiaries of the trust, this is treated as occupation by the trustees, who therefore have security of tenure and renewal rights.

Note that if the group company or the beneficiaries occupied as sub-tenants of other group companies or trustees respectively, the normal sub-tenancy and competent landlord provisions would operate and there would be no scope for s 42 or s 41(2) (see *Meyer v Riddick* [1990] 18 EG 97 on beneficiaries as sub-tenants).

2.11 PARTNERSHIPS: ASSIGNMENT WITHOUT ASSIGNMENT

Where the tenant is a group of individuals in partnership, whether only with each other or with others in whom the lease is not vested, and the premises are occupied for the purposes of a business carried on by the partnership, it will be those partners in whom the lease is vested on whom notices must be served, since they alone have the right to renew.

It frequently happens that partners retire from the business carried on at the premises but the lease is not assigned. In such a case, s 41A of the Act provides that notices must be served on or by those of the tenants who for the time being carry on the business, and only they will have the right to renew.

EXAMPLE

A business is carried on by A, B and C in partnership. A, B and C take a lease, or an assignment of a lease, and carry on the business from the premises demised.

D and E join the partnership and A and B retire. Therefore, the business is carried on by C, D and E, but the premises are still let to A, B and C.

On renewal, notices can only be served on or by C, who alone is liable for payment of rent and the discharge of any other obligations following the end of the contractual term while the tenancy continues under s 24 of the Act. Only C can take a new lease.

There is some protection for a landlord in s 41A(6), which gives the court jurisdiction to grant a new lease either to those of the original partners who remain in the partnership, or to them jointly with those others who carry on the business, and also to require guarantees, sureties or other conditions to be met having regard to the omission of the other original joint tenants from the persons who will be the tenants under the new tenancy. In the example above, the court could grant a new lease to C only, or to C, D and E and, if it considered such a requirement was equitable, it could require A and/or B to guarantee the new lease.

2.12 THE INSOLVENT LANDLORD

By s 67 of the Act, where the interest of the landlord is subject to a mortgage and the following conditions are satisfied, anything authorised or required to be done by, to or with, the landlord is deemed to be authorised or required to be done by, to or with, the mortgagee.

The conditions are:

– the mortgagee is in possession; or

– a receiver appointed by the mortgagee (or by the court) is in receipt of the rents and profits of the property.

Note that this will apply to receivers appointed under the Law of Property Act 1925 and to administrative receivers. It will not apply where an administrator has been appointed, and would only apply to a landlord in liquidation if a receiver had been appointed as well.

It follows that, where these conditions apply, notices must be served by or on the mortgagee and the mortgagee must be a party to any proceedings for a new tenancy.

Note that s 40(3) of the Act are specifically excluded from these provisions. A landlord is therefore required to respond to a tenant's Section 40 Notice, whether or not a receiver has been appointed over the property or over the whole of the landlord's assets and whether or not a mortgagee has taken possession of the property.

Note also that the fact that a receiver has been appointed does not necessarily mean that the landlord will want the renewal procedure to drift so as to minimise costs, even if this was possible. If the value of the property would be enhanced by locking in a higher income from a new lease, the receiver may have every interest in speeding up the renewal.

Chapter 3

THE TENANT'S POSITION

3.1   TENANT'S REQUEST FOR A NEW TENANCY UNDER SECTION 26

The tenant can precipitate matters by serving his own notice requesting a new tenancy under s 26 of the Act. He need not wait for the landlord to serve a Section 25 Notice first, provided that he has a fixed term of at least one year.

A Section 26 Request must be in the prescribed form, or in a form substantially to the like effect, and set out the proposed commencement date of the new tenancy, a date no earlier than expiry of the contractual term. It must be served on the competent landlord no less than 6 months and no more than 12 months before the proposed commencement date. In certain circumstances it must be served on the competent landlord's mortgagees: see **2.12**.

A copy of the prescribed form is included in Appendix 1.

The effect of a Section 26 Request is that the proposed commencement date stated in the request becomes the termination date of the existing tenancy.

The landlord must serve a counter notice within 2 months of receiving a Section 26 Request if he intends to oppose the request for a new tenancy, in which case the counter notice must state on which s 30 ground the landlord will rely (s 26(6)). The possible grounds are set out at **4.1**.

There is no prescribed form of landlord's counter notice, but a form is printed by law stationers for use when the landlord objects to a new tenancy, and a copy of this is included in Appendix 1. Counter notice may be given by letter so long as the essential information is given – whether or not the landlord objects to a new tenancy and if so on which of the s 30 grounds.

The permitted methods of service correspond to those available to the landlord, for which see **2.7**.

Whether or not a counter notice has been served by the landlord, the tenant must make a court application for a new tenancy. Under the new law (ie if the tenant's Section 26 Request was made on or after 1 June 2004) the tenant may make a court application for a new tenancy:

–   not less than 2 months after service of the Section 26 Request, and no later than the proposed commencement date of the new tenancy;

–　　but if the landlord serves a counter notice objecting to renewal (under s 26(6)), then the tenant can apply to the court for a new tenancy at any time after that counter notice is given, again up to and including the proposed commencement date of the new tenancy. In other words, if the landlord objects to renewal, that brings forward the date when the tenant can apply to court.

(These new time limits are in s 29A of the Act).

This is another radical change from the old law under which the tenant had to make his court application not less than 2 and not more than 4 months after service of the Section 26 Request. We will have to keep these old time-limits in mind for several years, while cases to which the old law applies continue to be active.

If the tenant is minded to delay issuing proceedings, he has to remember that the landlord can now start the ball rolling by applying to the court himself, at any time up to the day immediately before the proposed commencement date of the new tenancy.

3.2　TENANT'S TACTICS

Under the old law it was often argued (not least in previous editions of this book) that if the landlord failed to serve a full 12-month Section 25 Notice then the longer the wait the more likely that the tenant could benefit from delaying by serving a 12-month Section 26 Request because by doing so the tenant could gain for himself a longer period at the old rent. Against this was (and still is) the risk that the landlord could serve a Section 25 Notice at any time.

> EXAMPLE
>
> Lease will expire 24 December 2005.
>
> Landlord has not served Section 25 Notice before 25 March 2005.
>
> Tenant could serve Section 26 Request on 26 March 2005 extending the lease (at the old rent) until 25 March 2006, but decides to wait in the hope of a longer period at the old rent.
>
> Landlord serves Section 25 Notice on 1 April 2005, terminating the lease on 24 December 2005.

While it is still true under the new law that postponing the termination of the old lease also means postponing the start of the full new rent, this is much less likely to benefit the tenant because of changes made by the RRO to interim rent calculation and procedures. Under the new law, either the landlord or the tenant can apply for interim rent which will be payable from the earliest date which could have been specified in the Section 25 Notice or in the Section 26 Request, as the case may be. Also, where the renewal was not opposed and the tenant is granted a new tenancy of the whole of the premises comprised in the current tenancy, under the new law the interim rent will normally be the rent payable under, and at the commencement of, the new tenancy (s 24C(2)), ie without any discount. The result of these changes is that, in practice, the tenant will not gain for himself a longer period at the old rent.

For more comments about interim rent, see Chapter 8.

If the market rent is lower than the existing contractual rent, and the tenant wants to take a new lease, it will usually be in the tenant's interests to seize the initiative by serving a Section 26 Request as early as possible so that he can make his application to the court for a new tenancy at the earliest possible date. He will then be able to maximise pressure on the landlord by pushing the court procedures as a background to negotiation.

A Section 40 Notice may also be used by the tenant to establish who the competent landlord is. The tenant must know on whom to serve his Section 26 Request and whom to name as respondent to any subsequent application. However, this will prove counter-productive because the landlord will then be alerted to serve a Section 25 Notice with the shortest possible period. In most cases, the tenant will serve a Section 26 Request and a Section 40 Notice together, to gain the benefit of surprise.

Copies of the prescribed forms of tenant's Section 40 Notice are included in Appendix 1.

3.3   SECTION 26 AND TENANT'S BREAK CLAUSES

When market rents fell during the recession of the early to mid 1990s, there were suggestions that a tenant fortunate enough to have a break clause also had a relatively risk-free way of reducing his rent, by exercising the break clause and then claiming a new lease under the Act.

The main argument against this was that s 24(2), which states that a business tenancy shall continue unless terminated in accordance with the provisions of the Act, will not prevent the business tenancy coming to an end by notice to quit given by the tenant. Section 69(1) defines notice to quit as a notice to terminate a tenancy given in accordance with the provisions of that tenancy. Therefore, a Section 26 Notice served after a contractual break notice would not be effective.

The question was then asked whether a Section 26 Request could in itself be a contractual break notice. It cannot: *Garston v Scottish Widows* [1996] 23 EG 131.

Therefore a tenant who exercises a contractual option to determine but really wants to stay takes the risk that his landlord will be happy for him to go.

3.4   SECTION 25 NOTICE AND THE TENANT

The new law is a lot simpler than the old law.

Under the new law, ie after receiving a Section 25 Notice on or after 1 June 2004:

–   the tenant does not need to serve a counter notice at all;

–   the tenant may make a court application for a new tenancy at any time up to and including the date specified in the Section 25 Notice.

It is worth setting out the rules under the old law, since renewal proceedings to which it applies will continue for several years and there may be claims that the time-limits were not complied with.

After receiving a Section 25 Notice, the first step for the tenant was to serve a counter notice indicating that he did not intend to give up possession. This had to be given in writing no more than 2 months after the giving of the Section 25 Notice. If the tenant failed to give a counter notice, he lost his right to a new tenancy.

There was no prescribed form for a tenant's counter notice but a form was published by law stationers.

In a case where the tenant's solicitors erroneously served a counter notice stating that the tenant was willing to give up possession and then, within the 2-month time-limit, tried to correct their error by serving another counter notice stating that the tenant was not willing to give up possession, it was held that the second counter notice was valid: *Pennycook v Shaws (EAL) Limited* [2003] EWHC 2769 (Ch); [2003] 3 EGLR 28. The High Court accepted that there could be cases where the tenant had given a positive representation that it would give up possession and the landlord had acted to its detriment on the basis of that representation, creating an estoppel preventing the tenant from issuing a second counter notice. That would depend on the facts of each case.

The tenant then had to apply to the court for a new tenancy no less than 2 months and no more than 4 months after service of the Section 25 Notice.

3.5   TENANT'S TIME-LIMITS – WARNING

The wording of s 29 of the Act is absolute: an application for a new tenancy shall not be entertained unless the time-limits for counter notice and application are met. An application made too early is not valid (*Stevens & Cutting Ltd v Anderson* [1990] 11 EG 70).

The RRO introduced a new s 29B into the Act, specifically allowing the time-limit for the issue of proceedings to be extended (ie allowing the application to court to be made after the termination date specified in the Section 25 Notice or the day immediately before the commencement date requested in the Section 26 Request).

The landlord and tenant may agree before such a date to extend the period within which an application to the court must be made.

They may also agree further extensions, but any agreement for a further extension must be made before the end of the period specified in the current agreement.

When agreements are made to extend the period, the Section 25 Notice or Section 26 Request are to be treated as terminating the tenancy at the end of the period specified in such an agreement, or, if there are a series of agreements, specified in the last agreement.

The Act does not require such agreements to be made in writing. From a tenant's point of view, it would be very foolish to rely on an agreement which was not documented in writing.

It is again worth setting out the rules under the old law, since renewal procedures to which it applies will continue for several years and there may be claims that a court application was made too late (or too early: an application made too early was not valid: *Stevens and Cutting Limited v Anderson* [1990] 11 EG 70).

Under the old law, there was nothing in the Act allowing an extension of the time-limits. It was said that the landlord may consent to an extension of the time-limits, or may be estopped from taking the point that the time-limits have not been complied with, by continuing with the renewal procedure as if there had been compliance. In principle, it seemed correct that if a landlord had indicated that he would not object to a new lease being granted after some procedural error by the tenant, he should have been estopped from objecting to renewal solely because of the procedural error, but the cases usually quoted to support the possibility of estoppel were not in fact decided on that basis.

(1) *Bristol Cars Ltd v RKH (Hotels) Ltd (in liquidation)* (1979) 38 P & CR 411: Section 26 Notice was served in February 1976 and landlord did not claim it was invalid until April 1977 – landlord was estopped, but this was not a case on time-limits.

(2) *Kammin's Ballrooms Co Ltd v Zenith Investments (Torquay) Ltd* [1971] AC 850:
     tenant's application was defective, but landlord was not estopped because
     it had opposed the grant of a new tenancy throughout.

(3) *Stevens & Cutting Ltd v Anderson* [1990] 11 EG 70: tenant's application was
     made too early in August 1985, but the point was not taken until October
     1987 – landlord was not estopped because it had opposed the grant of a
     new tenancy throughout.

(4) *Salomon v Akiens* [1993] 14 EG 97: a new lease had been agreed 'subject to
     lease' and the tenant did not apply to the court – because all negotiations
     had been 'subject to lease' – landlord was not bound to grant a new lease in
     the terms so agreed and was not estopped from taking the point that no
     application had been made and the tenant had no right to remain in
     occupation after the expiry of the contractual term.

Claims by tenants that their solicitors' failure to comply with the time-limits has
lost them their right to a new tenancy were one of the greatest sources of
negligence claims against solicitors. With fewer and more flexible time-limits
under the new law, there should be far fewer claims.

3.6   DIARY DATES FOR TENANT AFTER SECTION 25 NOTICE

Diarise 2 months before the date specified in the Section 25 Notice to check
whether an application to court should be made, then one month before, then
2 weeks before – and always diarise the specified termination date itself.

If there is an agreement under s 29B to extend the period, diarise corresponding dates leading up to the expiry date of that agreement.

Be particularly careful if there are last minute negotiations to extend the time
for the service of proceedings. There are bound to be some landlords
somewhere who will try to string their tenants along by appearing to consider a
request for an extension right up to the last minute, in the hope that the tenant
will be too confident and miss the time-limit.

If the tenant has exercised his rights under the 1927 Act to make improvements
(see Chapter 11), the claim for compensation should be made within 3 months
of service of the Section 25 Notice. The tenant should check at the outset
whether this will apply and then diarise 3 months less 2 weeks and finally 3
months less one week from the date of the notice to make this claim. Note that
the tenant will not be entitled to compensation under the 1927 Act if he renews
his lease under the 1954 Act.

3.7 DIARY DATES FOR TENANT AFTER SECTION 26 NOTICE

Diarise 2 months plus one week after the date of the notice as the first date for making the application to court for a new tenancy with reminders. Then diarise 2 months before the date specified in the Section 26 Request to check whether an application to court should be made, then one month before, then 2 weeks before – and always diarise the specified date itself.

If there is an agreement under s 29B to extend the period, diarise corresponding dates leading up to the expiry date of that agreement.

Be particularly careful if there are last minute negotiations to extend the time for the service of proceedings. There are bound to be some landlords somewhere who will try to string their tenants along by appearing to consider a request for an extension right up to the last minute, in the hope that the tenant will be too confident and miss the time-limit.

If the tenant has exercised his rights under the 1927 Act to make improvements (see Chapter 11), the claim for compensation should be made within 3 months of the date on which the landlord gives counter notice or, if he does not give a counter notice, within 3 months of the latest date on which he could have done so. Therefore, when the Section 26 Request is served, diarise 2 months plus 2 weeks from the date of the request to check whether the landlord has served a counter notice and diarise 5 months less 2 weeks and finally 5 months less one week from the date of the request to check the position. Once a counter notice has been received, diarise 3 months less 2 weeks and finally 3 months less one week from the date of the request itself to check the position and make the claim if necessary. It is important that the two sets of dates are not confused because the latest date if a counter notice had not been served will obviously be later than the relevant date if it had.

3.8 TENANT'S RESPONSE TO DEFECTIVE SECTION 25 NOTICE

As stated at **2.6** above, some defects in a Section 25 Notice will not automatically make it invalid.

Therefore, it is never advisable simply to ignore a Section 25 Notice even if the tenant believes it to be so flawed that it is invalid. The appropriate action under the old law was to serve a counter notice specifically without prejudice to the tenant's claim that the Section 25 Notice was not valid (in *Keepers and Governors of the Free Grammar School of John Lyon v Mayhew* [1997] 17 EG 163 the Court of Appeal recommended this as the prudent course).

If the tenant received a defective Section 25 Notice but served a counter notice and then issued proceedings for a new tenancy without challenging the defective notice, it may have been estopped from challenging it later – this was the position in the *Mayhew* case.

Of course, the tenant does not need to serve a counter notice at all under the new law. However, we would still suggest that an apparently invalid Section 25 Notice should be challenged before an application is made to the court for a new tenancy, in the hope that this will defeat any estoppel argument.

The tenant may wish to accompany a rejection of the landlord's Section 25 Notice by his own Section 26 Request. There is an obvious (and painful) trap. An address is given for correspondence at the foot of the Section 25 Notice, which will usually be the landlord's solicitors' address. However, a Section 26 Request cannot validly be served on anyone other than the landlord unless the tenant can prove that the other people on whom it was served had actual authority to receive it, or can prove that the landlord actually became aware of it. Any Section 26 Notice served in these circumstances therefore should be served on the landlord with a copy to its solicitors.

3.9   NOTICES AND PENDING LAND ACTIONS

The lease which is being renewed will either be registered at the Land Registry in its own right, or will not (either because it is too short to be capable of substantive registration or because no events have occurred which required it to be registered) in which case it will be an overriding interest. The continuation tenancy under the Act will have the same status. However, technically speaking, the tenant's proceedings for a new tenancy will be a pending land action which by s 87 of the Land Registration Act 2002 is not an overriding interest.

It follows that the tenant's solicitors should make an index map search against the address of the property as soon as they are instructed and should register a unilateral notice (if the landlord's title is registered) or a pending land action (if the landlord's title is unregistered) as soon as the application for a new tenancy is made.

Any such registrations must, of course, be withdrawn once the new lease has been completed or court proceedings for a new tenancy are discontinued.

Chapter 4

GROUNDS FOR OPPOSITION

4.1 PERMITTED GROUNDS

The seven permitted grounds of opposition to a new tenancy are clearly set out in s 30(1) of the Act. They are as follows:

(a) where, under the current tenancy, the tenant has any obligations as respects the repair and maintenance of the holding, that the tenant ought not to be granted a new tenancy in view of the state of repair of the holding, being a state resulting from the tenant's failure to comply with the said obligations;

(b) that the tenant ought not to be granted a new tenancy in view of his persistent delay in paying rent which has become due;

(c) that the tenant ought not to be granted a new tenancy in view of other substantial breaches by him of his obligations under the current tenancy, or for any other reason connected with the tenant's use or management of the holding;

(d) that the landlord has offered and is willing to provide or secure the provision of alternative accommodation for the tenant, that the terms on which the alternative accommodation is available are reasonable having regard to the terms of the current tenancy and to all other relevant circumstances, and that the accommodation and the time at which it will be available are suitable for the tenant's requirements (including the requirement to preserve goodwill) having regard to the nature and class of his business and to the situation and extent of, and facilities afforded by, the holding;

(e) where the current tenancy was created by the sub-letting of part only of the property comprised in a superior tenancy and the landlord is the owner of an interest in reversion expectant on the termination of that superior tenancy, that the aggregate of the rents reasonably obtainable on separate lettings of the holding and the remainder of that property would be substantially less than the rent reasonably obtainable on a letting of that property as a whole, that on the termination of the current tenancy the landlord requires possession of the holding for the purposes of letting or otherwise disposing of the said property as a whole, and that in view thereof the tenant ought not to be granted a new tenancy;

(f) that, on the termination of the current tenancy, the landlord intends to demolish or reconstruct the premises comprised in the holding or a substantial part of those premises or to carry out substantial work of construction on the holding or part thereof and that he could not reasonably do so without obtaining possession of the holding (if the landlord uses this ground, the court can sometimes still grant a new tenancy if certain conditions set out in s 31A of the Act can be met);

(g) that, on the termination of the current tenancy, the landlord intends to occupy the holding for the purposes, or partly for the purposes, of a business to be carried on by him therein, or as his residence (the landlord must normally have been the landlord for at least five years to use this ground).

Those most commonly encountered are (f) and (g).

4.2   SECTION 30(1)(f): INTENTION TO DEMOLISH OR RECONSTRUCT

In order to establish a valid ground of opposition under s 30(1)(f) the landlord must intend to:

–   demolish or reconstruct the whole of the premises; or

–   demolish or reconstruct a substantial part of the premises; or

–   carry out substantial works of construction on the whole or part of the premises, which could not reasonably be carried out without obtaining possession.

Reconstruction has been held to include rebuilding works involving a substantial interference with the structure of the building, although structure should not necessarily be confined to outside or load-bearing walls (*Romulus Trading Co Ltd v Henry Smith's Charity Trustees* [1990] 32 EG 41). The same case held that the works have to be looked at as a whole, and that preparatory and ancillary works are relevant.

The question whether proposed works are 'substantial' is a question of fact and degree. The Court of Appeal refused to overturn a decision in the county court that proposed works confined to the ground floor of a property on three floors which would have involved the removal of the existing shop front, its replacement by an arcade entrance and the removal of a wall at the back did not constitute a reconstruction of a substantial part of the premises (*Atkinson v Bettison* [1955] 1 WLR 1127). The Court of Appeal accepted that works did amount to substantial works where the landlord proposed to amalgamate two shops, involving putting in a new shop front, changing the means of access from the street, removing three-quarters of the dividing wall and replacing it with screens and some demolition and construction works to the WCs (*Bewlay (Tobacconist) Limited v British Bata Shoe Co Limited* [1959] 1 WLR 45) and where the landlord proposed to alter a ground floor shop with two storage rooms at the rear and a yard behind them into a single enclosed space to be used as an amusement arcade, involving the removal of all the brick walls, their substitution by rolled steel joists at roof level, lowering the floor by eight inches and installing a new shop front (*Joel v Swaddle* [1957] 1 WLR 1094). More recently, works to convert a 60-bedroom hotel with communal bathrooms into a four star hotel with 38 en suite bedrooms, involving the removal of internal stud partition walls, the addition of new walls and a lift, the removal of part of the roof, new openings in existing walls and the restoration of a staircase, all of which were expected to take 12 months to carry out at a cost of some £2m, were held in the County Court not amount to 'substantial works of construction' and the High Court refused to overturn that decision on appeal (*Marazzi v Global Grange Limited* [2002] EWHC 3010 (Ch); [2003] 34 EG 59).

The landlord must prove that he has decided to carry out the works and that there is a reasonable prospect, or a real chance, of the works being carried out – a prospect that is strong enough to be acted on by a reasonable landlord (*Aberdeen Steak Houses Groups Limited v The Crown Estate Commissioners* [1997] 31 EG 101, quoting the Court of Appeal case of *Cadogan v McCarthy & Stone Developments Ltd* [1996] EGCS 94).

The landlord must show a firm and settled intention at the date of the hearing (*Betty's Cafes Ltd v Phillips Furnishing Stores Ltd* [1959] AC 20). Intention is objectively assessed by the court and it is a question of fact. It follows that it is whoever is the competent landlord at the date of the hearing who must have the intention to carry out the work (*Marks v British Waterways Board* [1963] 1 WLR 1008). It does not matter that the identity of the competent landlord has changed since the Section 25 Notice was originally given, nor does it matter that the landlord who gave the notice had no intention to redevelop, so long as that notice specified ground (f) as a ground of objection. An intention to grant a long lease to a proposed developer in conjunction with a building agreement will satisfy the test of intention (*Gilmoor Caterers Limited v St Bartholomew's Hospital Governors* [1956] 1 QB 387). Therefore, a landlord wishing to sell a site ripe for redevelopment can pass the benefit of a Section 25 Notice objecting on ground (f) to a purchasing developer.

Evidence of the landlord's intention can be given in person by an individual landlord (*Mirza v Nicola* [1990] 30 EG 92). Where the landlord is a company a board resolution is preferable (*Espresso Coffee Machine Co Ltd v Guardian Assurance Co Ltd* [1959] 1 WLR 250) but if the board does not have sufficient powers a shareholders' resolution will be necessary (*A & W Birch Ltd v P B (Sloane) Ltd* (1956) 106 LJ 204). The landlord may also give an undertaking to the court which, because breach of it would be a contempt of court, is perfectly decisive of fixity of intention (*Espresso Coffee*).

Intention includes a reasonable prospect of being able to carry out the work at the end of the tenancy – in view of s 64 of the Act this is in practice 4 months after the hearing – and that ability includes planning consent and funding (*Reohorn v Barry Corporation* [1956] 1 WLR 845 and, more recently, *Edwards v Thompson* [1990] 29 EG 41). In *Edwards v Thompson*, the landlord had planning permission which included other land with a condition that no part of the development was to be occupied until the whole had been completed; although the landlord had plans, funds and a contractor to redevelop the tenant's land, she had not agreed terms to acquire the other land, nor was funding yet in place for the main development and it was not likely that the development of the remainder of the entire site would be ready to proceed on the termination of the tenancy. The court held that ground (f) was not established. Contrast *London Hilton Jewellers Ltd v Hilton International Hotels Ltd* [1990] 20 EG 74, where the landlords were able to carry out proposed works in stages, and had the means to do so. Note also that there is no absolute rule that prospective illegality will prevent a landlord from establishing an intention to demolish and reconstruct. In *Palisade Investments Ltd v Colln Estates Ltd* [1992] 27 EG 134, the prospective illegality was that the outline programme of works produced to the court would have involved a breach of the conservation area consent obtained by the landlord. However, the Court of Appeal accepted that there was evidence that the landlord could and would resolve this.

The landlord's need for possession must be considered in the light of s 31A(1), which states that the landlord cannot establish the requisite need for possession if:

(1) the tenant is willing for the new tenancy to include a right of entry which allows the landlord access and necessary facilities to carry out the proposed works, so long as, given that access and those facilities, the work would not interfere with the tenant's business user to a substantial extent or for a substantial time; or

(2) where the tenant will accept a tenancy of an economically separable part of the premises and either possession of the rest of the premises is reasonably sufficient to enable the works to be carried out, or (1) above applies to the economically separable part. A part is deemed economically separable only if, after the work is completed, the aggregate of rents obtainable on separate lettings of that part and the remainder of the premises would not be substantially less than the rent which would be reasonably obtainable on a letting of these premises as a whole.

The landlord will not of course be able to rely on ground (f) if rights of entry for redevelopment in the old lease are sufficiently wide to allow him to carry out the work which he proposes because a new lease could be granted incorporating these rights which would allow the work to be carried out. A tenancy of a petrol station which reserved to the landlord rights to enter 'for the purposes of carrying out such improvements, additions and alterations to the service station' as the landlord considered reasonable after consulting with the tenant was held sufficiently wide to include total demolition and replacement by a new design of petrol filling station (*Price v Esso Petroleum Co Limited* (1980) 255 EG 243). In another petrol station case, the tenant operated a petrol station and a garage for the sale and repair of motor vehicles. The landlord intended to demolish all the existing buildings, construct new pipe islands with a new canopy over them and new buildings to contain the control area, shop, office, store, staff room and toilets, and a car wash. This would involve removing the existing facility for the sale and repair of motor vehicles. The lease included covenants by which the tenant allowed the landlord to enter and carry out 'any improvement or addition to or alteration of the premises which the landlord may consider desirable', and also a covenant forbidding the tenant to use the property other than as a filling and service station together with the sale and repair of motor vehicles without the landlord's consent. The Court of Appeal held that although the lease was wide enough to allow the landlord to enter the premises and carry out the work, the effect of him doing so would have been to deprive the tenant of the facilities needed to carry on its business and that in turn would have placed the landlord in breach of its covenant not to derogate from its grant. Therefore the landlord required not only physical possession but also legal possession to carry out the works it proposed and ground (f) was upheld (*Leathwoods v Total Oil (Great Britain) Limited* (1984) 270 EG 1083).

Where a property is clearly ripe for redevelopment but the landlord either has not decided how to redevelop it or is for some other reason not ready to redevelop, one tactic would be to serve Section 25 Notices which do not object to renewal and then argue for the grant of a short lease or the inclusion of a break clause in a longer lease so that the position can be considered again within a relatively short time. This will delay payment of compensation, and may avoid it altogether if the tenant leaves to seek premises with greater security. See Chapters 5 and 10.

4.3   SECTION 30(1)(g): INTENTION TO OCCUPY

The landlord cannot rely on ground (g) if he purchased the property during the 5 years preceding the termination date (ie the date set out in the Section 25 Notice or Section 26 Request) and at all times since the purchase there has been a tenancy or succession of tenancies to which the Act applies (ie if the reversion was purchased 4 years prior to termination, occupied by the purchaser for one year and then let for 3 years, ground (g) would be available).

The 5-year rule will be satisfied by a landlord whose interest consists of a series of successive leases, the earliest of which began before the start of the 5-year period (*Artemiou v Procopiou* [1966] 1 QB 878) and by a landlord which held a freehold interest at the beginning of the period and carried out a sale and leaseback, creating an overriding lease, during the period (*VCS Car Park Management Limited v Regional Railways North East Limited* [2000] 1 EGLR 57).

There is an exception to the 5-year rule for companies within a group (see **2.10** for comments on the definition of a group of companies). By s 42(3) of the Act where the reversion is held by a member of a group:

–   the requisite intention to occupy includes occupation by any other member of the group for the purposes of a business carried on by that member; and

–   purchase of the reversion from, or creation of a reversionary interest by, another member of the group will not be counted for the 5-year rule.

Where the landlord has a controlling interest in a company, ground (g) is available whether it is the landlord himself or that company who wishes to occupy the property in order to carry out a business (s 30(1A), replacing similar provisions formerly in the now deleted s 30(3)). Under the new law, where the landlord is a company and somebody has a controlling interest in that company, ground (g) can be used if either the company or that person wants to occupy the property. These new rights for somebody with a controlling interest in a corporate landlord will not apply if: first, he purchased the controlling interest during the 5 years preceding the termination date (ie the date set out in the Section 25 Notice or Section 26 Request); and secondly, at all times since the controlling interest was acquired there has been a tenancy or succession of tenancies to which the Act applied (s 30(1B) and (2A) introduced by the RRO).

The landlord's intended occupation must be for business purposes but need not be personal and can be with a partner (*Re Crowhurst Park* [1974] 1 All ER 991), through a manager (*Chez Gerard Ltd v Greene Ltd* (1983) 268 EG 575), through an agent (*Teesside Indoor Bowls Ltd v Stockton on Tees Borough Council* [1990] 46 EG 116), or through a company controlled by the landlord (*Harvey Textiles Limited v Hillel* (1979) 249 EG 1063). There must be a genuine intention to occupy the premises for the landlord's business purposes and a reasonable prospect that the landlord will be able to bring this about by his own act of volition (*Gregson v Cyril Lord Ltd* [1963] 1 WLR 41) but the second part of this test is only used to determine the reality of the landlord's intention, not the probability of his achieving its start nor its prospects of ultimate success. To put it another way, 'the test is whether the landlord has a reasonable prospect of achieving his genuine intention of occupying the demised property for the purpose of conducting a business there within a short or reasonable time after termination of the tenancy': *Dolgellau Golf Club v Hett* [1998] 2 EGLR 75.

The Court of Appeal has held that these two tests – genuine intention and real possibility – do not have to be considered sequentially. If the landlord has no genuine intention to run the business, it is not necessary to investigate the reality or the fantasy of the landlord's business plan. If the landlord has no prospect of succeeding in his aim of starting a business, there is no need to investigate the landlord's bona fides (*Zarvos v Pradhan* [2003] EWCA Civ 208; [2003] 26 EG 180).

The date on which these tests must be met is the date of the hearing, as with ground (f). This is illustrated in the Court of Appeal case *Ambrose v Kaye* [2002] 1 EGLR 49. In that case, the landlord was claiming possession under ground (g) on the basis that he had a controlling interest in a company which wanted to operate a business at the property (under the old s 30(3)). In closing submissions at the end of the trial, the tenant's solicitor advocate took the point that there was no evidence the landlord had a controlling interest in the company. There was then a short adjournment, during which the landlord's wife transferred to him sufficient shares in the company to give him a controlling interest. The court then allowed a further adjournment to allow this to be established by documentary evidence, which in due course the landlord did. The tenant's appeal that the county court judge should not have exercised his discretion to allow these adjournments was rejected.

The landlord does not need to intend to occupy the whole of the property immediately so long as he can show an intention to occupy a substantial part within a reasonable time after the end of the tenancy (*Method Development Limited v Jones* [1971] 1 WLR 168). However, Lord Denning once said that the ground will not be established where the landlord intends to occupy merely for a short period before selling (*Willis v British Commonwealth Universities' Association* [1964] 2 All ER 40).

Chapter 5

THE NEW LEASE: THE PROPERTY AND TERMS

5.1 THE PROPERTY COMPRISED IN THE NEW LEASE

The tenant's right is to a new lease of those parts of the premises originally let to him which he occupies for the purposes of his business, or which companies within the same group occupy for the purposes of their business, defined in the Act as the holding (s 32(1)).

However, the landlord can insist that the tenant takes a new lease of the whole of the premises or leaves. Then the court has no discretion, ie it must make an order for a new tenancy of the whole of the premises (s 32(2)). The tenant's protection (such as it is) is either to discontinue proceedings once the landlord's intentions are clear or to make use of s 36(2) of the Act which allows a tenant 14 days after the court has made an order for a new tenancy to apply for it to be revoked.

5.2 VARIATION OF TERMS

The leading case as to the terms to be included in the new lease is *O'May v City of London Real Property Co Ltd* [1982] 1 All ER 660, which lays down the following guidelines.

(1) The party proposing a variation to the terms of an old tenancy must show a reason for doing so.

(2) If the proposed change is made, will the party resisting it be adequately compensated by a consequential adjustment in the rent?

(3) Will the proposed change materially impair the tenant's security in carrying out his business or profession?

(4) Taking all relevant matters into account, is the proposed change fair and reasonable between the parties?

Elsewhere in the judgments, the policy of this part of the Act is summarised as follows:

'... the court must begin by considering the terms of the current tenancy ... the burden of persuading the court to impose a change in those terms against the will of either party must rest on the party proposing the change ... the change proposed must, in the circumstances of the case, be fair and reasonable and should take into account, amongst other things, the comparatively weak negotiating position of a sitting tenant requiring renewal, particularly in conditions of scarcity, and the general purpose of the Act which is to protect the business interests of the tenant so far as they are affected by the approaching termination of the current lease, in particular as regards his security of tenure.'

Note that s 35(2) of the Act allows the court to include among the relevant circumstances it takes into account when deciding the terms of the new tenancy the provisions of the Landlord and Tenant (Covenants) Act 1995 (ie the abolition of privity of contract for tenants) (see **5.8**). Section 34(4) of the Act requires the court to take into account when determining the rent payable under a new tenancy any effect on rent of the operation of the provisions of the Landlord and Tenant (Covenants) Act 1995.

The introduction to the *Code of Practice for Commercial Leases* (Second Edition) recommends that landlords and tenants 'should have regard to the recommendations of this Code when they negotiate lease renewals'. However, that Code does not have the force of law and therefore cannot vary the terms of the Act. As its introduction goes on to acknowledge: 'Under current legislation if a court has to fix terms for a new lease it may decide not to change the terms from those in the existing lease'.

5.3 DURATION AND LANDLORD'S BREAK CLAUSES

Under the new law, the court may grant such period of up to 15 years as is considered reasonable in all the circumstances. Under the old law, the maximum period was 14 years. This is a very wide discretion, but there have been some guidelines.

Where a tenant wants only a short lease his wishes are likely to be met, on the basis that the purpose of the Act is to protect the tenant's security of tenure, not the landlord's investment value (*CBS United Kingdom Ltd v London Scottish Properties Ltd* (1985) 2 EGLR 125, where the tenant had requested a little more than 2 years against the landlord's request for a full 14 years – the tenant was successful).

Where property is 'ripe for redevelopment' but the landlord is not yet ready, the court is likely to grant either a short lease or to insert a relatively early break clause, on the basis that 'It is not the policy lying behind Part II of the 1954 Act to permit the rights of the tenant under the new tenancy to stand in the way of reconstruction and redevelopment of commercial property; the test is whether there is a real possibility (as opposed to a probability), that the premises in question will be required for reconstruction during the continuance of the proposed new tenancy': *National Car Parks Ltd v The Paternoster Consortium Ltd* [1990] 15 EG 53. In that case the real possibility that vacant possession of the area of the Paternoster Square redevelopment would be obtained within 10 years was held to justify the inclusion of a break clause operable at any time, even though no application for planning consent had yet been made.

If the court decides to include a break clause in the new lease, it has discretion to decide how early in the term it can be exercised. Here are a few illustrations:

–   In *Adams v Green* [1978] 2 EGLR 46 where the landlord had no plans for redevelopment but wished to have flexibility, the Court of Appeal ordered a break clause operable on 2 years' notice.

–   In *JH Edwards & Sons Limited v Central London Commercial Estates Limited* [1984] 2 EGLR 103, the landlord had no settled redevelopment scheme, the court below had ordered a minimum term of 10 years and the Court of Appeal replaced this by a break clause exercisable after 5 years.

–   In *Amica Motors Limited v Colebrook Holdings Limited* [1981] 2 EGLR 62 the tenant motor dealer had invested heavily in adjoining premises when the landlord was not opposing a new tenancy. When the case came to trial, the landlord's position had changed. The trial judge ordered a break clause operable after 3 years and the Court of Appeal refused to overturn this.

–   In *Becker v Hill Street Properties Limited* [1990] 2 EGLR 78 the trial judge found that the landlord would be ready to redevelop after about one year but ordered the grant of a new tenancy for a term of 4½ years to coincide with the date of the tenant's planned retirement. The Court of Appeal supported this decision and said it was 'unthinkable' that the tenant should have less than 3 years' security of tenure.

–   More recently in *Davy's of London (Wine Merchants) Limited v The City of London and Saxon Land BV* [2004] EWHC 2224, the landlord proposed to carry out a comprehensive redevelopment of a site including the property in question. The High Court acknowledged that a tenant running a serious business needs to plan ahead, acknowledged that their duty was to balance the redevelopment aspirations of the landlord against the business interests of the tenant, supported the decision of the trial judge to order a renewal term of 14 years with a rolling redevelopment break clause and ordered that the first date on which the break clause could be operated would be a little less than 4 years after the date of the trial.

The principle of including a break clause is not restricted to cases where property is ripe for redevelopment in an objective sense; the test is what the landlord bona fide wants to do with his own premises: see *Adams v Green* and *Becker v Hill Street Properties Ltd.*

Note that the landlord will have to establish ground (f) to exercise the break clause.

5.4   GUARANTORS

The liability of guarantors under the old lease will not continue after the contractual expiry date (ie during continuation under the Act) unless the lease specifically so provides (*Junction Estates Ltd v Cope* (1974) 27 P & CR 482).

Of course it is possible to draft a surety covenant which will continue during this period and indeed during any renewal (it would even be possible to draft a specific obligation for the guarantor to enter into a renewal lease), but it would be extremely rare for any potential guarantor to accept such obligations.

Apart from a special provision relating to former partners (see **2.11**), there is no specific provision in the Act which entitles the court to require existing guarantors to become parties to the new lease. They are not themselves parties to the litigation and a failure to provide guarantors is not in itself a ground for refusing to grant a new lease (*Barclays Bank Ltd v Ascott* [1961] 1 WLR 717). However, it has been held that the new lease can include a term obliging the tenant to provide a satisfactory guarantor within a specified period (*Cairnplace Ltd v CBL (Property Investment) Company Ltd* [1984] 1 WLR 696).

5.5   FIXING THE INITIAL RENT

In practice, this is usually one of the first matters negotiated but under the Act it is the last matter to be decided, taking into account all the other terms which have been agreed or have been ordered by the court.

The basis is set out in s 34 of the Act as the rent at which, having regard to the terms of the tenancy (other than those relating to rent), the property might reasonably be expected to be let in the open market by a willing lessor but disregarding:

–   any effect on rent of the fact that the tenant or his predecessors have been in occupation;

–   any goodwill arising because of the carrying on at the property of the business of the tenant (whether by the tenant or by a predecessor in that business);

–   any effect on rent of any improvement which was carried out by the tenant (ie the person who was the tenant at the time the improvement was made) during the tenancy which is being renewed or, if carried out during an earlier tenancy, which was completed not more than 21 years before the application for this renewal was made so long as at all times since the improvement was carried out the part of the property affected by it has been comprised in business tenancies at the termination of which the tenants did not quit (for example, if the work was carried out 15 years ago, and 10 years ago a business tenant voluntarily left the property and there was a new letting to a separate business tenant, the improvement will not be disregarded; but, if 10 years ago, the old business tenant renewed and then assigned his lease the improvement will be disregarded). Improvements will not be disregarded if they were carried out in pursuance of an obligation to the immediate landlord, however recently they were carried out. Neuberger J suggested in *Durley House Limited v Cadogan* [2000] 1 EGLR 60 that the requirement for the improvement to have been carried out by the tenant may well not be satisfied where a third party has carried out the work unless the tenant has been involved in identifying, supervising and/or financing the specific improvements.

The Court of Appeal has recently held in *J Murphy and Sons Limited v Railtrack plc* [2001] EWCA Civ 679; [2002] 1 EGLR 48, that s 34(1) of the Act contains all the essential guidance needed for the determination of the rent, with the specific statutory disregards which it includes, and that no other disregards should be implied. In that case, the tenant owned the freehold of the land surrounding the holding but its lease did not contain any rights of way. The trial judge had discounted the new rent because the holding was landlocked, despite the fact that the tenant obviously had no difficulty getting to or from it, and the Court of Appeal upheld that decision.

The court will decide the new rent on the basis of evidence of comparable transactions, to be given by surveyors acting as expert witnesses who may not only give evidence of the comparable transactions, but also express opinions on how they should be interpreted. In recessionary times, the headline rent may be misleading and the court has a duty at least to attempt to break down any package into terms of open market rental valuation (*French v Commercial Union* [1993] 24 EG 115).

Note also in relation to expert witnesses that their duty is to the court, not to the party which instructs them, to give independent assistance by way of objective unbiased opinion regarding matters within their expertise (a form of words used in *National Justice Compania Naviera SA v Prudential Assurance* [1993] 2 Lloyd's Rep 68). This case law has been codified in the Civil Procedure Rules 1998 (CPR, r 35.3).

5.6 RENT REVIEW

The court has power to include provisions for rent review as one of the terms of the new tenancy: s 34(2) of the Act. Since rent reviews are now universal in the open market when leases for more than 5 years are granted, it can be assumed that the court could be persuaded to exercise this power when ordering the grant of a new lease for a term of more than 5 years. It is less clear whether the court will order upwards-only reviews, or reviews which can go either upwards or downwards.

Rent review clauses allowing the rent to rise or fall were included by the High Court in *Stylo Shoes Ltd v Manchester Royal Exchange Ltd* (1967) 204 EG 803 and *Janes (Gowns) Ltd v Harlow Development Corporation* (1979) 253 EG 799. In the latter case, evidence was given to the court of a new development to be built nearby which was likely to reduce rental values in the immediate neighbourhood.

Rent review clauses allowing the rent to rise or fall have also been awarded in three county court cases. They are *Boots The Chemists Ltd v Pinkland Ltd* [1992] 28 EG 118, *Amarjee v Barrowfen Properties Ltd* [1993] 30 EG 98 and *Forbuoys plc v Newport Borough Council* [1994] 24 EG 156. *Blythwood Plant Hire Ltd v Spiers Ltd (in receivership)* [1992] 48 EG 117 should be contrasted. In that case, an upwards-only rent review was awarded, with the judge commenting that neither of the valuers who gave evidence had any practical experience of an upwards or downwards rent review clause and that such clauses were virtually unknown in the real world until recently – an approach which sounds dated 13 years on. All four cases are, of course, not precedents even in other county courts.

It is relevant that none of the old leases in these cases contained rent review provisions (with the possible exception of *Forbuoys* where the report is silent), so the courts were not required to apply the *O'May* principles to the text of the review clause. Clearly, where an old lease includes an upwards or downwards rent review the landlord will bear the burden of justifying a change to an upwards-only review, and vice versa.

Landlords will argue for upwards-only reviews on the basis that *Stylo Shoes* is out of date, *Janes (Gowns)* depended on special circumstances and the county court cases do not form any precedent. Tenants will argue that the reasoning in *Stylo Shoes* and *Janes (Gowns)* should be followed (as it was in three of the county court cases) and that *Blythwood* should be treated as a special case, because the landlord was in receivership with the receivers intending to market the landlord's interest immediately, evidence being produced that the absence of an upwards-only review would reduce the value of that interest. Tenants may also seek support from Recommendation 6 of the *Code of Practice for Commercial Leases* (Second Edition) which recommends that landlords should offer alternatives to upwards only rent reviews priced on a risk-adjusted basis, and argue that if the court orders an upwards and downwards review, the court will take that into account when fixing the new rent.

Whether the parties agree on the form of a rent review clause or it is incorporated by the court, it is essential that improvements are properly dealt with. As explained at **5.5**, voluntary improvements carried out within the previous 21 years where there has been a continuous series of business tenancies will not be taken into account when fixing the initial rent. This is useful but of course the lease should also make sure that they will be disregarded on all rent reviews during the term.

5.7   REPAIRS, REINSTATEMENT AND ALTERATIONS

If the repairing covenant in the old lease simply required the tenant to keep the property in repair, therefore implying that the tenant was under no duty to put it into any better condition than it was at the time of letting, a landlord may be prejudiced by accrued dilapidations. Once a new lease with the same form of repairing covenant is completed, the tenant will no longer be obliged to make good any dilapidations which existed when the new lease was granted. A landlord can protect himself either by serving a Schedule of Dilapidations prior to completion of the new lease or by insisting that the new lease contains a 'put and keep' repairing obligation, requiring the tenant to improve the property from its initial condition. The threat of a Schedule, particularly if the old lease contains provisions allowing the landlord to recover the cost of preparing and serving it and all other costs in connection with it, is frequently enough to achieve an adequate repairing covenant.

Alternatives to the above are the inclusion of a specific provision that for the purposes of the repairing covenant the property shall be deemed to be in the state and condition in which it was on the date of the previous lease (which may be unenforceable in practice if no Schedule of Condition was taken at that time) or a specific declaration that any breach of the old lease which existed on the date the new lease was completed shall be treated as a breach of the new lease.

Where a licence for alterations has been granted during the term of the old lease, a landlord must consider very carefully whether any reinstatement obligations contained in the licence will continue to be enforceable once the old lease has been replaced by a new lease. It will usually be prudent to incorporate specific obligations in the new lease requiring the tenant to reinstate alterations specified by reference to the licence which authorised them (for example, 'on or before the expiration of the term hereby granted [unless requested by the landlord not to do so] to reinstate the demised premises to the state and condition in which they were prior to the carrying out of alterations authorised by a Licence dated (   ) and made between (   )').

5.8   IMPACT OF THE LANDLORD AND TENANT (COVENANTS) ACT 1995

As stated at **5.2**, the Landlord and Tenant (Covenants) Act 1995 ('the 1995 Act') introduced a new s 35(2) of the Act which specifically entitles the court to take the 1995 Act into account when determining the terms of the new lease and the rent payable. This reflects the fact that any lease now granted by the court will be a new lease for the purposes of the 1995 Act and therefore the tenant will automatically be released from any continuing liability under that lease after a lawful assignment.

Section 35(2) does not specify *how* the court is to take the effect of the 1995 Act into account. In the First Edition of this book, the authors argued that the court would be likely to accept that it was the policy of the 1995 Act to allow the parties at least to specify the circumstances in which consent to assignment could be withheld and to specify conditions which a landlord could impose within which he would automatically be deemed to be acting reasonably, and in doing so the court would follow current market practice at the time of any trial.

The first significant reported decision on these provisions, *Wallis Fashion Group Limited v CGU Life Assurance Limited* [2000] 2 EGLR 49, did not accept this argument. The issue in that case was whether the new lease should contain a condition giving the landlord the right to insist on receiving an 'Authorised Guarantee Agreement' from the outgoing tenant on any application for consent to an assignment whether or not this was reasonable, as the landlord wished, or whether this condition precedent should have a reasonableness qualification as the tenant proposed. Neuberger J decided the case in favour of the tenant and remarked:

> 'I do not think that the terms of s 35 of the 1954 Act, as interpreted in *O'May* entitled the landlord to say that, on a renewal under the 1954 Act, he should be given as generous terms as the 1995 Act provides. The 1995 Act represents a sea-change in the law relating to a tenant's liability after he assigns the lease, and it also alters the law relating to the landlord's power to impose terms on assigning the lease. It does not merely represent a sea-change in what had been common practice, but in what a landlord can lawfully require, both in terms of what is to be included in the lease initially and what he can demand upon an assignment.'

The case concerned a shop in a centre where 18 leases were being renewed at roughly the same time. Two of the tenants abandoned their applications to renew, 15 of the renewals were settled by agreement and only one of them actually reached the county court. Of the 15 renewals which were settled by agreement, 14 of the tenants had approved the clause in question in the form the landlord wanted, and the landlord claimed the one exception had been an oversight on its part. The landlord argued that this showed market forces had produced a covenant in the form wanted by the landlord. More controversially, Neuberger J did not regard this as conclusive:

'... it is to be borne in mind that each of the other tenants in the present case may not have regarded this point as one worth holding out for if all the other issues were agreed ... Many tenants may be prepared to concede a particular point in negotiations because it is not a point of great importance in relation to a particular case, but the landlord is prepared to insist on it, as he has far wider interests.'

The authors were disturbed by this argument at the time and still are. The court has to take into account what is reasonable between the parties, and it had always been understood in practice that evidence of what was being generally accepted in the market would count as evidence of what was reasonable between the parties. If that is not accepted, it is difficult to see what evidence of what is reasonable can be produced and how fairness between the parties can be assessed other than by the subjective opinions of the particular judge.

Wallis Fashion was a county court case. As such it is not a precedent even in the other county courts. However, it was decided by a prestigious High Court judge and the authors believe it is likely that Neuberger J's general remarks will be followed.

Grounds to withhold consent

Examples of possible circumstances which a landlord may wish to specify as grounds allowing him to withhold consent include:

(1) where (in the reasonable opinion of the landlord) the assignee is not of sufficient financial standing to enable him to pay the rent and comply with the tenant's other obligations in the lease – the general ability to perform test;

(2) where the assignee cannot pass a specified profits or net assets test (for example, a requirement that post-tax profits in each of the last 3 years are more than three times the rent reserved, or that the net assets of the company are more than three times the aggregate of the rents that were reserved) – a financial test;

(3) where the ability of the proposed assignee to meet his obligations under the lease is, or might reasonably be considered to be, [substantially] less than that of the current tenant – a comparative status test;

(4) where (in the reasonable opinion of the landlord) the value of the landlord's reversionary interest would be diminished or otherwise adversely affected by the proposed assignment – a damage to the reversion test;

(5) where the assignee is an associated company of the outgoing tenant;

(6) if at the date of request for consent the outgoing tenant has not paid the rents due under the lease and/or has not substantially observed and performed its covenants in the lease;

(7) where the assignee enjoys diplomatic status or State immunity.

Conditions

Examples of conditions which a landlord may wish to have a right to impose include:

(1) the payment of all rents and other sums due prior to the date of assignment;

(2) the outgoing tenant guaranteeing his successors' obligations under an authorised guarantee agreement as defined in the 1995 Act (after *Wallis Fashion* the courts can be expected to include a reasonableness qualification; a landlord in a strong negotiating position may still wish to press for an absolute requirement);

(3) the assignee providing personal guarantors and/or a rent deposit;

(4) the obtaining of any consents required from a superior landlord and/or a mortgagee;

(5) payment of the landlord's costs.

Advice to landlords

In the authors' experience, drafting practice during the first few months after the 1995 Act came into force was to include as many circumstances in which consent could be withheld and preconditions as the draftsmen could devise, possibly motivated by a fear that any court considering the general issue of reasonableness might be persuaded that a landlord should not be entitled to take into account a circumstance or condition which he had failed to specify in the original draft.

A report by the Association of British Insurers (ABI) Working Party on the 1995 Act recommended that, whilst every situation had to be looked at on its own merits so that different conditions could be implied in different circumstances, they did not as a general rule advocate use of the financial tests or a comparative status test but recommended reliance on a general ability to perform test and saw some merit in a damage to the reversion test.

The authors have seen institutional landlords gradually pulling away from imposing detailed conditions, and either following the ABI recommendations or relying on the general law of reasonableness, a trend which the decision in *Wallis Fashion* will surely encourage. Note also the possible impact of onerous provisions at rent review. In theory, the more restrictions there are on the assignability of the hypothetical lease, the more likely the hypothetical tenant will be to reduce its rental bid – thus reducing the uplift on review. Landlords may seek to avoid this by provisions that the hypothetical lease will not include some or all of the restrictions on assignment in the actual lease but tenants will always resist this strongly, and as it does not seem to be (and is not likely to become) market practice, it is unlikely that a court would incorporate such provisions into a review clause on a statutory renewal. A landlord may also seek to mitigate difficulties by arguing for a distinction between provisions prejudicing an actual tenant and the effect of such restrictions on a hypothetical tenant. For example, while a comparative status test will restrict the range of potential assignees for a substantial actual tenant, it will not necessarily restrict the market for assignment by a hypothetical tenant who was of lesser status.

Taking all this into account, the authors' advice to landlords is broadly to follow the ABI recommendations and to seek to incorporate:

–   a general ability to perform test;

–   a damage to the reversion test;

–   an express statement that all tests operate without prejudice to the right of the landlord to withhold consent on any other grounds where such withholding of consent would be reasonable;

–   a requirement that the outgoing tenant must enter into an Authorised Guarantee Agreement as defined by the 1995 Act if it is reasonable for the landlord so to require.

Advice to tenants

Tenants should strongly resist the imposition of any of the tests except:

–   a general ability to perform test;

–   an obligation to enter into an Authorised Guarantee Agreement as defined by the 1995 Act limited to cases in which it is reasonable for the landlord so to require.

Tenants may wish to refer to Recommendation 9 of the *Code of Practice for Commercial Leases* (Second Edition) that the only restriction on assignment of the whole premises should be obtaining the landlord's consent (which is not to be unreasonably withheld) unless 'the particular circumstances of the letting justify greater control'. Landlords will no doubt claim that every letting contains such particular circumstances.

Financial tests should be resisted on the grounds that they are normally too inflexible. Whilst such a test may be reasonable as one of a number of factors to be taken into account, it is unreasonable for a landlord to preclude a prospective assignee on the grounds that it fails to pass any particular financial test.

Similarly, a comparative status test should be rejected on the grounds that it too may be inappropriately inflexible and substantially restrict the marketability of a lease.

If a landlord insists on maintaining a certain level of covenant, as opposed to relying upon a level of covenant which would pass the general ability to perform test, the most flexible additional test which it may be reasonable to agree is the damage to the reversion test. Adopting that, the incoming tenant would not be obliged to meet some arbitrary financial test nor to match the covenant status of the outgoing tenant, but simply must not be of such lower status that the value of the reversion is actually affected. On this basis, the tenant could require the landlord to take account of any other relevant factors, for example guarantees or deposits offered.

If a landlord insists on imposing a tenant's breach test, this should only be accepted if it refers to substantial breaches.

5.9   ESSENTIAL TERMS: ADVICE FOR TENANTS

In a falling market where supply exceeds demand, a tenant who can credibly threaten to relocate is in an excellent position to negotiate good terms, whatever the contents of the old lease. In a rising market, where the landlord can be confident that evidence will justify a higher rent as time passes, a tenant may be willing to accept less than attractive terms in order to fix an acceptable rent. Among the essential provisions to consider are as follows.

(1)   *Length of term* (see **5.3**).

(2)   *Term commencement* (and, therefore, rent commencement). Where a lease renewal is decided by a full trial, the term and the new rent will not start until 4 weeks plus 3 months after the date of hearing – 4 weeks to appeal, plus the 3 months provided for by s 64 of the Act. Until that commencement date, the landlord will only be entitled to interim rent, but the level of the new rent will be fixed by reference to evidence available at the date of hearing. The tenant may be willing to agree a term commencement date on the date following the expiry of the old lease in return for an acceptable level of rent in a rising market (in practice, this is normally seen as fair by both parties).

(3)   *Initial rent* (see **5.5**).

(4)   *Rent review*: not only whether it should be upwards-only or either way (see **5.6**) but a tenant will also normally seek elimination of artificial and oppressive rent review provisions which allow the landlord to recover a 'headline rent'. The Court of Appeal has not been sympathetic to landlords attempting to achieve a headline rent, but in the four cases

reported together as *Co-operative Wholesale Society Limited v National Westminster Bank plc* [1995] 1 EG 111, a form of words providing for the rent review to generate a rent 'payable in respect of the premises after the expiry of a rent-free period of such length as would be negotiated in the open market between a willing landlord and a willing tenant upon a letting' was held to be sufficiently precise to achieve that result.

(5) *Insurance*: an acceptable list of risks against which the landlord covenants to insure (note in particular that acts of terrorism will probably not have been listed as a specific risk in leases more than 10 years old) preferably not limited by availability, cover at full reinstatement value (preferably with an objective test of that value) and, if possible, a landlord's covenant to make up any deficiency out of his own monies. The tenant will also seek to argue that any cesser of rent be unlimited in time; the landlord will equally seek to argue that it should be limited to the period of the landlord's loss of rent insurance. Market practice varies and the party seeking to justify a change from the terms of the old lease will normally find itself in difficulties.

(6) *Damage by uninsured risks*: particularly since 9/11, tenants have been very concerned about what would happen were their premises to be damaged or destroyed by risks against which insurance was either not available at all, or was available only on terms so onerous that the landlord was entitled, under the terms of its covenants, not to take out such insurance. In the traditional FRI lease, the tenant would be required to repair and reinstate (under its repairing covenant) while continuing to pay rent (because the cesser of rent would not have been triggered) without having any insurance moneys with which to do so. Put as starkly as that, the prospect is rarely acceptable! However, it must be acknowledged that the landlord whose income-generating asset has been destroyed and who will not receive any insurance moneys to rebuild it, is not exactly happy either. Exactly where the balance of risk should fall is a matter for negotiation, the result of which depends on the relative bargaining strength of the parties. It is often possible to agree a compromise along the lines that if there is damage or destruction by a risk against which the landlord was entitled not to insure and did not insure, the tenant should be able to exercise a break clause and walk away from the lease. Where the demise is of the internal surface within a structure which the landlord retains (a very common arrangement in multi-let buildings), so that it is physically impossible for the tenant to reinstate his demise unless and until the structure around it has been reinstated by somebody else, the tenant is in a strong position to argue that he should be able to walk away from the ruins with no continuing liability.

(7) *Service charge* (where appropriate): how the proportion is to be calculated and what it is to cover.

(8)   *Repairs* (see **5.7**).

(9)   *Alterations*: a tenant will normally seek freedom to carry out internal alterations without having to request his landlord's consent, subject to notifying the landlord at the time.

(10) *Alienation* (see **5.8**).

(11) *Permitted use*: a tenant will normally seek to achieve maximum flexibility (eg open Class A1 for a shop), but must remember that this in particular will increase the rental value.

(12) *Keep open* (normally only relevant to shops): a tenant will normally seek to exclude any positive obligation to occupy or trade from the property. Even though the House of Lords has ruled against granting a mandatory injunction to enforce such a covenant (in *Co-operative Insurance Society Limited v Argyll Stores (Holding) Limited* [1997] 23 EG 141), it is still possible that damages would be awarded.

(13) *Interest*: percentage above base rate and days of grace before payment is due. Even if there was no interest provision in the old lease, it is inconceivable that a court would refuse to include one now.

There are circumstances in which a tenant may be happy to retain an adverse obligation (for example, a requirement that a particular part of the property be used for storage or by a specific user (as in *Department of the Environment v Allied Freehold Property Trust Ltd* [1992] 45 EG 156)) in order to reduce the rental value of the new lease, and can use the *O'May* principles to its advantage.

Where a threat to relocate is not seen as credible, or a landlord is particularly stubborn, a tenant has to bear in mind that the *O'May* test will be applied by the court, with the party proposing a variation to the old terms bearing the burden of justifying that variation. It will not necessarily be enough simply to assert that the tenant would be able to negotiate the terms it is requesting in the current market (eg *Boots the Chemists Ltd v Pinkland Ltd*, where the county court declined to exclude a 'keep open' obligation which had been in the old lease, commenting that Boots had failed to discharge the burden of showing why it should not be incorporated into the new lease).

5.10   COSTS OF THE NEW LEASE

The Costs of Leases Act 1958 states that a tenant cannot be obliged to pay his landlord's costs in connection with the grant of a lease unless he agrees in writing to do so. The court will not deprive the tenant of this protection by writing such an obligation into the new lease (*Cairnplace Limited v CBL (Property Investment) Co Limited* [1984] 1 All ER 315).

If the old lease obliged the tenant to pay the landlord's costs in connection with the grant of any renewal lease, this will be treated as void, on the basis that it places a penalty on the tenant if he exercises his rights under the Act, which is void under s 38(1) of the Act (*Stevenson and Rush (Holdings) Limited v Langdon* (1979) 38 P & CR 208).

Chapter 6

THE NEW COURT PROCEDURES

6.1 CONTROL IN THE HANDS OF THE COURT

Commenting on court procedures for lease renewal through the three editions of this book has been rather like shooting at a moving target.

In the first edition of this book, this chapter's title 'Tactical Use of Court Procedures' reflected the fact that under the old court procedures for lease renewal there was scope for tactical positioning designed to give one party or the other a negotiating advantage.

The big change between the first and second editions was the introduction of the Civil Procedure Rules 1998 (CPR). These allowed less scope for the tactical use of court procedures.

The introduction of the CPR and supplementary Practice Directions in April 1999 was intended to encourage quicker, fairer and cheaper dispute resolution. Since their implementation, pre-action protocols have been established in order to bring about a change in the culture of dispute resolution. Parties are required actively to consider ways of resolving their differences without going to court. Litigation is to be a last resort. Where litigation proves unavoidable, the CPR shifted the ability to control the procedural timetable from the parties and their advisers into the hands of the court.

The change between the second and third editions of this book has been the introduction of CPR Part 56 which deals specifically with claims under the Act (and some other statutes relating to land) and a practice direction (PD56) supplemental to it.

Under the old law there was, and where it applies there will continue to be, a tension between the desire of most parties in most cases to negotiate at their own pace, and the activist intentions of the CPR.

The vast majority of lease renewals are essentially non-hostile litigation. Once the protective steps required by statute have been taken, the lawyers and their clients are usually content to wait for the respective surveyors to negotiate new terms. In such circumstances they would not want the court to force the pace of proceedings.

In cases to which the new law applies (ie those where the Section 25 Notice or the Section 26 Request was served or made on or after 1 June 2004) the parties are free to postpone issuing proceedings until the termination date specified in the Section 25 Notice or the date immediately before the commencement date requested in the Section 26 Request. They can also agree in writing to extend even this deadline (for previous comments on this, see Chapter 3). This would allow them, if they both wished to do so, to keep the matter out of the court's hands for as long as they like. Two parties who are content to negotiate at a speed of their choosing will not be faced with a judge ordering them to speed up.

This change in the law would also allow judges of an activist mind to argue that if one of the parties has applied to the court this must mean that party wants the court to take control of the 'dispute' and to impose its own timetable to resolve the 'dispute', as pressing on to trial as fast as possible. We may well see the courts taking a more active approach to the smaller number of cases coming before them.

6.2   HIGH COURT OR COUNTY COURT

The application for a new tenancy must be started in the county court (CPR r 56.2) unless 'exceptional circumstances' justify starting the claim in the High Court. (PD56, para 2.2). Those exceptional circumstances may include, in an appropriate case (PD56, para 2.4):

–   if there are complicated disputes of fact; or

–   if there are points of law of general importance.

The value of the property and the amount of any financial claim may be relevant 'but these factors alone will not normally justify starting the claim in the High Court' (PD56, para 2.5).

PD56, para 2.3 warns that if a claim is started in the High Court and the High Court decides the claim should have been started in the county court, it will normally either strike out the claim or transfer it to the county court on its own initiative, and will normally disallow the costs of starting the claim in the High Court and of any transfer.

Not surprisingly, the vast majority of cases will be started in the county court. This chapter assumes throughout that the litigation is taking place in the county court.

6.3   WHICH COUNTY COURT?

The claim must be started in the county court for the district in which the land is situated (CPR r 56.2). Court staff are often willing to confirm by telephone which court is the right court.

If the application is made to the wrong county court, the court staff must still issue it: *Gwynedd Council v Grunshaw* [1999] 4 All ER 304.

Where proceedings have been started in the wrong county court, a judge has power under CPR r 30.2 to do any of the following:

–   to transfer the proceedings to the correct county court;

–   to continue them in the county court in which they have been started; or

–   to strike them out.

An order to strike out the proceedings is not likely to be made except in extreme cases. The court is more likely to regard the issue of proceedings in the wrong court as a breach of a rule or practice direction which does not in itself invalidate the issue of those proceedings, and make an order to remedy the error under CPR r 3.10.

6.4   THE APPLICATION

Where the landlord does not oppose the grant of a new tenancy (which will be the majority of cases) the application for the new tenancy must be made under the procedure in Part 8 of the CPR.

In the minority of cases where the landlord does oppose the grant of a new tenancy, the application must be made under the procedure in Part 7 of the CPR. A landlord's application for the termination of a tenancy without renewal under the amended s 29(2) (which is of course only possible if the new law applies) must also use the Part 7 procedure.

Remember that in cases where the old law applies, it is only the tenant which can make the application. In cases to which the new law applies, either the landlord or the tenant can make the application.

Whether or not the landlord is opposing the grant of a new tenancy, the application must contain details of the following (PD56, para 3.4):

–   the property to which the claim relates;

–   the particulars of the current tenancy, including the date, the parties and the duration, the current rent and the date and method of termination;

–   every Notice or Request given or made under Sections 25 or 26; and

–   the expiry date of the period during which the application to the court
    could be made, or any agreed extension of it.

Where the application is being made by the tenant, the following details must
also be given (PD56 para 3.5):

–   the nature of the business carried on at the property;

–   whether the tenant claimant relies on the new s 23(1A) (occupation by a
    company in which the tenant has a controlling interest, or by a person with
    a controlling interest in the tenant company), s 41 (tenancies held on
    trust) or s 42 (the 'groups of companies' section) and if so, on what basis;

–   whether the tenant claimant relies on s 31(A) and is attempting to resist a
    landlord's objection on ground (f) by relying on s 31(A) (for more about
    this see Chapter 4);

–   whether any, and if so what part, of the property comprised in the tenancy
    is occupied neither by the tenant claimant nor by a person employed by
    the tenant claimant for the purpose of the tenant claimant's business;

–   the tenant claimant's proposed terms of the new tenancy; and

–   the name and address of anyone known to the tenant claimant who has an
    interest in the reversion (either now or in not more than 15 years) on the
    termination of the existing tenancy and who is likely to be affected by the
    grant of the new tenancy or, even if they do not meet this test, anyone who
    has a freehold interest in the property.

Where the claim is made by the landlord (which is possible if, but only if, the
new law applies) the following additional information is required (PD56,
para 3.7):

–   the landlord claimant's proposed terms of the new tenancy;

–   whether the landlord claimant is aware that the tenancy is one to which
    s 32(2) applies (ie where the immediate tenant occupies part, but not all,
    of the property comprised in the current tenancy for the purposes of its
    business) and, if so, whether the landlord claimant requires that any new
    tenancy shall be a tenancy of the whole of the property comprised in the
    current tenancy, or just of the holding (ie the part occupied by the tenant
    for the purposes of its business); and

–   the name and address of anyone known to the tenant claimant who has an
    interest in the reversion (either now or in not more than 15 years) on the
    termination of the existing tenancy and who is likely to be affected by the
    grant of the new tenancy or, even if they do not meet this test, anyone who
    has a freehold interest in the property.

Where the landlord is making an application (under Part 7) for the termination of a tenancy under s 29(2) as amended, the following additional information is required (PD56, para 3.9):

– the landlord's claimant's grounds of opposition;

– full details of those grounds of opposition; and

– the terms of a new tenancy that the landlord claimant proposes if his claim fails (in other words, even if the landlord objects to the grant of a new tenancy so strongly that he is willing to start the ball rolling himself, and even though it would be normal for the question whether or not the tenant should be granted a new tenancy to be decided as a preliminary issue, the claimant landlord must set out the terms he would offer if that claim failed).

Statement of Truth

The CPR require every application and statement of case (pleading) to include a statement of truth, namely: '[I believe]/[The claimant believes] that the facts stated in this [claim form] are true'.

Paragraph 3.1 of the Practice Direction supplementing CPR Part 22 requires the statement of truth to be signed by the party to the proceedings or by its legal representative on behalf of that party.

Where the claimant is a company, the statement of truth must be signed by a person holding a senior position in the company such as a director or other officer. The person signing the statement of truth must state the position or office he holds.

If the legal representative signs, he must do so in his own name but the statement will refer to his client's belief not his own. If the legal representative signs a statement of truth, that signature will be taken by the court as a statement that:

(1) the client on whose behalf he has signed has authorised him to do so;

(2) before signing he had explained to the client that in signing the statement of truth he would be confirming the client's belief that the facts stated in the document were true; and

(3) before signing he had informed the client of the possible consequences to the client if it should subsequently appear that the client did not have an honest belief in the truth of those facts.

Significantly in a lease renewal context, the Practice Direction goes on to state that an agent who manages property or investments for the party cannot sign a statement of truth.

The requirement for a statement of truth has made it more essential than ever to ensure applications are prepared in good time, so that they can be considered and verified by the client before being submitted to the court.

Issuing the application

CPR, r 6.3(3) requires the party who prepares a document for service by the court to file a copy for the court and sufficient copies for each party to be served. A cheque for the issue fee must also be submitted. This is currently £130.

An application is 'made' when the applicant has done everything required of him and the application is received by the court office, not when the process is subsequently issued by the court: *Aly v Aly* (1984) 128 SJ 65. Where the time fixed for making the application expires on a day on which the court office is closed, and for that reason it cannot be issued on that day, it will be in time if it is filed on the next day on which the court office is open: *Hodgson v Armstrong* [1967] 2 QB 299.

Service

The rules require service of the proceedings under the Act within 2 months from the date of issue: CPR, r 56(3).

The court has a limited discretion under CPR r 7.6(3) to extend time for service of the claim form if (but only if):

–   the court has been unable to serve the claim form; or

–   the claimant has taken all reasonable steps to serve the claim form, but has been unable to do so; and

–   in either case, the claimant has acted promptly in making the application.

Be warned that where the failure to serve within the 2-month period is a result of the failure of the claimant's solicitors to appreciate that the time for service is 2 months, rather than the normal 4-month period specified in CPR r 7.5(2), the failure to serve is likely to be fatal to the claim: *Chabba v Turbogame Limited* [2001] EWCA Civ 1073.

CPR, r 6.2 deals with methods of service and these include:

- personal service;

- first-class post;

- service via a document exchange; and

- service by fax.

Where the proceedings are served by the court, a notice is sent to the claimant confirming the date upon which service is deemed to have been effected. If the proceedings are served by the claimant, he must file a certificate of service within 7 days: CPR, r 6.14.

6.5 RESPONDING TO THE APPLICATION

Within 14 days of service of the claim form, the defendant on which it has been served must file an acknowledgement of service (CPR, r 10 for the general principle and CPR, r 8.3 specifically for claims under Part 8 (ie where the landlord does not object to the grant of a new tenancy)).

Where the claim is an unopposed claim and the application was made by the tenant, the landlord's acknowledgement of service must be in Form N210 and (by PD56, para 3.10) state the following:

- whether if a tenancy is granted the defendant landlord objects to any of the terms proposed by the claimant tenant and if so:

    the terms to which he objects, and
    the different terms which he proposes;

- whether the landlord is himself a tenant under a lease having less than 15 years unexpired at the date of termination of the claimant's current tenancy and, if he is, the name and address of any person who, to the landlord's knowledge, has an interest in reversion in the premises, whether immediately or in not more than 15 years from the termination date of the tenant's current tenancy, on the termination of the landlord's tenancy;

- the name and address of any person having an interest in the property who is likely to be affected by the grant of a new tenancy; and

- if the claimants tenant's current tenancy is one to which s 32(2) of the Act applies (ie where the tenant only occupies part of the demise for the purposes of its business) whether the defendant landlord requires that any new tenancy should be a tenancy of the whole of the property comprised in the tenant's current tenancy. See **5.1** above for a summary of s 32(2) of the Act.

Where the claim is an unopposed claim and the claimant is the landlord, the tenant's acknowledgement of service must be in Form N210 and must (by PD56, para 3.11) give details of the following:

–   the nature of the business carried on at the property;

–   whether the tenant relies on the new s 23(1A) (occupation by a company in which the tenant has a controlling interest, or by a person with a controlling interest in the tenant company), s 41 (tenancies held on trust) or s 42 (the 'groups of companies' section) and if so, on what basis;

–   whether any, and if so what part, of the property comprised in the tenancy is occupied neither by the tenant nor by a person employed by the tenant for the purpose of the tenant's business;

–   the name and address of anyone known to the tenant who has an interest in the reversion (either now or in not more than 15 years) on the termination of the existing tenancy and who is likely to be affected by the grant of the new tenancy or, even if they do not meet this test, anyone who has a freehold interest in the property; and

–   whether, if a new tenancy is granted, the tenant objects to any of the terms proposed by the landlord and if so:

>   the terms to which he objects, and

>   the different terms which he proposes.

Where the landlord opposes renewal and the claimant is the tenant the acknowledgement of service must be in Form N9 and must (by PD56, para 3.12) include details of the following:

–   the defendant landlord's grounds of opposition, with full details;

–   whether if a new tenancy is granted the defendant landlord objects to any of the terms proposed by the tenant and if so:

>   the terms to which he objects, and

>   the different terms which he proposes;

–   whether the landlord is himself a tenant under a lease having less than 15 years unexpired at the date of termination of the claimant's current tenancy and, if he is, the name and address of any person who, to the landlord's knowledge, has an interest in reversion in the premises, whether immediately or in not more than 15 years from the termination date of the tenant's current tenancy, on the termination of the landlord's tenancy

–   the name and address of any person having an interest in the property who is likely to be affected by the grant of a new tenancy; and

- if the claimants tenant's current tenancy is one to which s 32(2) of the Act applies (ie where the tenant only occupies part of the demise for the purposes of its business) whether the defendant landlord requires that any new tenancy should be a tenancy of the whole of the property comprised in the tenant's current tenancy. See **5.1** above for a summary of s 32(2) of the Act.

Where the landlord has made an application for the termination of the current tenancy without renewal under the amended s 24(2) of the Act (which, of course, can only be the case if the new law applies) then the tenant's acknowledgement of service must be in form N9 and must (by PD56, para 3.13) give details of the following:

- whether the defendant tenant relies on the new s 23(1A) (occupation by a company in which the tenant has a controlling interest, or by a person with a controlling interest in the tenant company), s 41 (tenancies held on trust) or s 42 (the 'groups of companies' section) and if so, on what basis;

- whether the defendant tenant relies on s 31(A) and is attempting to resist a landlord's objection on ground (f) by relying on s 31(A) (for more about this see Chapter 4);

- the terms of the new tenancy which the defendant tenant would propose if the landlord's application to terminate the current tenancy without renewal fails.

6.6   INTERIM RENT

The old law allowed a landlord to apply for an interim rent payable from the later of:

- the termination date specified in the landlord's Section 25 Notice or the tenant's Section 26 Request; or

- the date upon which the application for interim rent is made.

Where the old law applies, the court has no power to backdate an application for interim rent and no discretion to determine the date from which it should run.

Where the new law applies, either the landlord or the tenant can apply for interim rent and it is payable, by the new s 24B, from the earliest date of termination that could have been specified in the landlord's Section 25 Notice or the earliest date for the commencement of the new tenancy which could have been specified in the tenant's Section 26 Request.

See Chapter 8 for more detail about interim rent.

Applying for interim rent in the county court

Where proceedings for the grant of a new tenancy, or the termination of an existing tenancy without renewal, have already been commenced, the claim for interim rent must (by PD56, para 3.17) be made in one of the following ways:

– in the claim form; or

– in the acknowledgement of service or the defence; or

– by application on notice under Part 23 of the CPR.

If an application is made for interim rent under the new s 24D(3) of the Act (in other words, if the court has made an order for the grant of a new tenancy and an order for interim rent, but either the order for the grant of the new tenancy is revoked or the landlord and tenant agree not to act on it, so that a new interim rent has to be determined), that application must (by PD56, para 3.18) be made by an application or notice under Part 23 in the original proceedings.

Where no proceedings have (yet) been started for the grant of a new tenancy or the termination of an existing tenancy without renewal or where such proceedings have been started and have been disposed of (so that, in either case, there are no current renewal proceedings) then an application for interim rent must (under PD56, para 3.19) be made under the Part 8 procedure on a claim form which includes details of:

– the property to which the claim relates;

– the particulars of the relevant tenancy, including date, parties and duration, and the current rent;

– every Notice or Request given or made under ss 25 or 26;

– if the relevant tenancy has terminated, when and how it terminated;

– if the relevant tenancy has been terminated and a new tenancy has been granted, particulars of that new tenancy, including the date, parties, duration and rent and also in a case where s 24C(2) of the Act applies but the claimant seeks a different interim rent under s 24C(3), particulars and matters on which the claimant relies in order to invoke s 24C(3). (For more details on the different ways of calculating interim rent under the new law, see Chapter 8.)

6.7   FIXING A DATE FOR THE FIRST HEARING

County court

When the CPR was introduced, CPR Sch 2, CCR Ord 43, r 2(2) required the court to fix a date for the case management hearing of the proceedings when issuing (what was then always) the tenant's application.

In the authors' experience, most county courts did not do this and instead continued the pre-CPR practice of listing a case management conference on a 'date to be fixed'.

CPR Sch 2, CCR Ord 43 is no longer in force and the rules have been largely brought into line with common practice. Where the landlord does not oppose renewal, CPR r 56.3(3)(c) provides that the court will give directions about the future management of the claim after receiving the acknowledgement of service.

6.8   AGREEING DIRECTIONS

The rules encourage the parties to liaise in order to agree directions for the management of the case which they can then ask the court to order. If the court agrees with the directions suggested by the parties, it may make an order by consent without the need for a hearing.

It is important to check in advance with the court concerned whether a district judge will still require someone to attend a case management conference even where agreement has been reached because there is, as yet, no uniformity of approach.

CPR, r 29.3 provides that where a party has a legal representative the case management conference must be attended by a representative familiar with the case and with sufficient authority to deal with any issues that are likely to arise. It is now very rare for personal attendance to be required at a case management conference under the Act; they are usually dealt with by post or by telephone conference.

What will be included in the directions for the management of the case?

Where renewal is opposed by the landlord and the ground of opposition is a live issue, there will be a direction that the validity of that ground be tried as a preliminary issue so that further directions and a hearing on the terms of the renewal lease will only be necessary if the ground of opposition fails or is withdrawn.

Otherwise, in cases where the principle of renewal is unopposed a common (although by no means standard) form of order will usually include provisions in a form similar to the following.

(The suggestions below have been heavily influenced by the suggested Standard Directions drawn up by the Property Litigation Association and publicly available on their website. At the time of writing, the most recent version was the June 2003 revision; this is acknowledged to be out of date in some respects and is undergoing review.)

(1) The landlord shall serve on the tenant the draft Lease by no later than 4.00pm on a specified date. (Where appropriate, the direction may require this to be done in electronic form, either by email or on a computer disk.)

(2) The tenant shall serve on the landlord its proposed amendments marked in red or by schedule by no later than 4.00pm on a specified date (typically, 14 days after receipt of the draft) (if the original was served in electronic form by e-mail or on a computer disk, the direction might require the response also to be in an electronic form with the changes shown either in italics or underlined).

(3) The landlord shall by no later than 4.00pm on a specified date (typically 2 weeks after the receipt of the tenant's response) notify the tenant which amendments, if any, are disputed and specify the landlord's additional amendments marked in green (if the tenant's amendments were marked in red) or by counter-schedule (if the tenant's amendments were by schedule) (again, if exchange of documents has been in electronic form the direction may provide for this also to be done in electronic form).

(4) Each party shall by 4.00pm on a specified date give standard disclosure to all other parties by list.

Standard disclosure is the procedure by which parties to an action disclose to the others documents coming within the definition contained in CPR, r 31.6.

Standard disclosure is defined by r 31.6 as requiring a party to disclose only:

(a) the documents on which he relies;

(b) the documents which:

    (i) adversely affect his own case,
    (ii) adversely affect another party's case, or
    (iii) support another party's case; and

(c) the documents which he is required to disclose by a relevant Practice Direction.

In practice, standard disclosure in unopposed renewals is usually straightforward as each party will have seen relevant title documents, notices and open correspondence, and is often omitted.

Where the landlord is opposing renewal on redevelopment or own-occupation grounds, the disclosure exercise will be an important part of the proceedings. The landlord will normally be ordered to supply its list before the tenant supplied its list. The landlord's list should contain documents dealing with:

– the landlord's title to the site;

– the form of the intended development indicating the scope of the intended works;

– measures taken to obtain planning consent and comply with any conditions attached to consents or permissions;

– the financial viability of the proposed scheme and the landlord's ability to finance it; and

– appointment documents of the landlord's consultants including architects, engineers and quantity surveyors.

Some documents are privileged from disclosure. There are several categories of privilege including:

– communications between a solicitor and his client for the purpose of giving or obtaining legal advice;

– communications between a solicitor and third parties and the client created after litigation is contemplated or started; and

– without prejudice communications.

Labelling a document 'without prejudice' will not automatically protect that document from disclosure. The document will only be privileged from production to the extent that its contents are part of an attempt to negotiate an agreement or settlement of disputed points.

The new standard form list of documents must include a statement by the party giving disclosure:

– setting out the extent of the search that has been made to locate documents which he is required to disclose;

– certifying that he understands the duty to disclose documents; and

– certifying that to the best of his knowledge he has carried out that duty.

The statement must also expressly state that the disclosing party believes the extent of the search to have been reasonable in all of the circumstances.

Relevant factors when deciding the reasonableness of a search include:

– the number of documents involved;

– the nature and complexity of the proceedings;

– the ease and expense of retrieval of a particular document; and

– the significance of any document likely to be located during the search.

(5) Requests for inspection or copies of documents to be made by a specified date (usually 7 days after the date for disclosure).

(6) Each party shall serve on the other party the witness statements of all witnesses of fact on whom it intends to rely. There shall be simultaneous exchange of such statements by no later than 4.00pm on a specified date.

(7) The parties/the solicitors for the parties, are to meet/speak by 4.00pm on a specified date on a without prejudice basis with a view to narrowing the issues between the parties on the lease terms. The parties do, by no later than 4.00pm on a specified date, prepare and serve a schedule setting out such terms of the draft lease as are not agreed. In each case, the party seeking materially to depart from the terms of the current lease must set out its reasons for doing so.

(8) If the rent [and interim rent] for the new lease is not agreed between the parties, each party is to be at liberty to call one expert valuation witness at the hearing of the application for a new tenancy. Their reports, including lists of comparables and photographic evidence (if any) relating to the rent payable under the new lease are to be exchanged by no later than 4.00pm on a specified date. Such reports are to be agreed if possible.

(9) [In the rare cases where the parties are unable to agree the text of the lease: if the terms of the lease are not agreed between the parties, experts' reports are to be exchanged no later than 4.00pm on a specified date and agreed if possible, and if not agreed, such expert evidence is to be limited to one conveyancing expert for such party.]

(10) The respective experts are to meet/speak by 4.00pm on a specified date on a without prejudice basis with a view to narrowing the issues between the parties. The experts [or, where appropriate, the parties] are to agree a joint statement indicating those parts of the experts' evidence with which they are and are not in agreement (including as to facts, the description of the premises, any plans and photographs and the comparables (and any

plans and photographs relating to them)) with reasons, such statement to be served on all parties by no later than 4.00pm on a specified date.

CPR Part 35 deals with expert evidence. Whilst the above direction envisages each side appointing its own expert, the court can now impose a single expert on the parties without their consent being necessary: CPR, 35.7. A single expert is not a new concept. The RSC gave the court power to appoint a single expert but only on the application of one of the parties. In practice, such applications were rare.

If the parties cannot agree on a single expert, then the court may require the joint preparation of a list of experts with one to be chosen from that list. In the continued absence of agreement, the court has power to select an expert in such manner as it thinks fit. With unopposed renewals this is likely to involve asking the President of the RICS to make a suitable appointment.

It had been anticipated that unopposed lease renewals, where expert evidence does not relate to issues of liability but rather to quantum, ie rental value, would be well-suited to being dealt with by a single expert. In our experience, parties are reluctant to agree to submit issues of rental value to a single expert and this is rarely ordered.

Where two experts have been ordered, the court can still limit the amount of the expert's fees that the party instructing him is able to recover from the other party. The conduct of the party will be relevant in this context as the court considers the reasonableness of all issues pursued by the experts.

If the court directs a single joint expert to be used, each party gives the expert instructions, simultaneously sending a copy of those instructions to the other party: CPR, r 35.8. In practice, instructions prepared in these circumstances become more detailed than would otherwise be the case and in some cases have started to look more like submissions to an arbitrator.

CPR, r 35.10 requires the expert to state in his report the substance of all material instructions, whether written or oral, on the basis of which the report was written. Those instructions are no longer privileged against disclosure. However, in relation to those instructions, the court will not order disclosure of any specific document or permit any questioning in court other than by the party who instructed the expert unless there are reasonable grounds to consider the expert's statement of instructions to be inaccurate or incomplete. It is important to bear in mind that the instructions in which privilege is lost are only those which are 'material' and on the basis of which the expert's final report was written. Earlier drafts of the expert's report and instructions upon which earlier drafts were prepared will remain privileged.

It is possible for the parties to put written questions to the single expert, or where two experts have been ordered, to the other side's expert. These questions can only be put once, for the purpose of clarification of the report, and within 28 days of service of the expert's report: CPR, r 35.6. An expert's answer to such questions should be treated as part of his report.

In cases where a single joint expert has been ordered, it is usual to find that both sides instruct their own expert to review the single expert's report and advise as to any questions to be put to the single expert. Therefore, an order for one expert invariably ends up, in practice, with three experts becoming involved.

The Court of Appeal has considered the circumstances in which a party should be able to call additional expert evidence where a single joint expert had produced a report with which one of the parties was dissatisfied: *Walker v Daniels* [2000] 1 WLR 1382. The Court of Appeal concluded that in substantial cases (which the present case was) the joint instruction of a single expert should be seen as the first step in obtaining expert evidence and, subject to the discretion of the court, a party may still call his own evidence where he disagrees with the evidence of the joint expert. However, the Court of Appeal was not prepared to accept the argument that a refusal to allow the dissatisfied party to call his own expert conflicted with the right to a fair trial guaranteed by the European Convention on Human Rights. The view of the Court was that it would be unfortunate if case management decisions involved the need to refer to authorities from the European Court of Human Rights. This is likely to prove the first of many attempts to test the CPR by reference to the Human Rights Act 1998.

Paragraph 1 of the Practice Direction to CPR Part 35 deals with the form and content of an expert's report.

Finally, it is important to be aware of the timing of any order for expert evidence. With the swifter progress generally of unopposed renewal proceedings it is possible that an order will require exchange of expert evidence before the valuation date. This is obviously to be avoided if possible.

Under CPR, r 35.12, the court is able to direct a discussion between experts at any stage for the purpose of requiring the experts to:

–   identify the issues in dispute in proceedings; and

–   where possible, reach agreement on an issue.

It is likely that a meeting between experts would be useful before exchange of reports as well as after.

The rules confirm that the content of the discussion between the experts cannot be referred to at trial unless both parties agree; and that an agreement reached at a meeting of experts is not binding unless and until the parties expressly agree to be bound.

(11) Each party must file a completed listing questionnaire by no later than 4.00pm on a specified date with experts' reports, statements of issues by experts and witness statements.

This case [including the claim for interim rent] is to be tried as a fixture before a Circuit Judge in the period commencing on a specified date and ending on a specified date with a provisional time estate of [insert here an estimate of the length of the hearing].

The listing questionnaire is sent by the court to the parties, usually approximately 3 weeks before the date stipulated in the order for its return.

The information required to be provided in completing the listing questionnaire includes:

– whether or not the parties have complied with all previous directions and if not, why not;

– whether or not any further directions are required;

– whether or not permission to use written and oral expert evidence has been given or is requested;

– the name and field of expertise of the experts or single joint expert in question;

– whether or not the experts have met to discuss their report;

– any dates during the trial window when the experts will be unavailable to attend a trial;

– details of witnesses of fact and dates within the trial window when those witnesses will not be available;

– whether or not any witness statement has been agreed;

– details of legal representation at the trial; and

– a time estimate as to length of the trial and estimate of the number of pages of evidence to be included in the trial bundle.

The parties are required to file an estimate of costs when returning their listing questionnaires and the claimant is required to pay a listing fee.

Upon receipt of the completed listing questionnaire, the court considers whether it is necessary to list a pre-trial review or listing hearing.

On a pre-trial review or listing hearing, the court will make any further orders considered necessary for the efficient conduct of the trial.

Matters likely to be considered at this stage include:

–   whether to grant permission to give expert evidence orally;

–   the preparation and filing at court of a trial bundle and timescale for doing so (this will normally require a bundle to be filed between 3 days and 7 days prior to the trial date);

–   whether skeleton arguments are required to be filed prior to the trial; and

–   confirmation of the running order of the trial.

6.9   OFFERS TO SETTLE

Calderbank letters

A party to proceedings can try to exert some pressure on the other party by seeking to influence the court's discretion on costs by making an offer 'without prejudice save as to costs'; also known as a '*Calderbank* letter'.

An effective *Calderbank* letter should:

(1) be marked 'without prejudice save as to costs';

(2) contain an offer which is capable of acceptance;

(3) prove to have been an offer to settle on terms which, for the recipient of the offer, are as good as or better than the basis ultimately ordered by the court.

If a party rejects an offer contained in a *Calderbank* letter and subsequently achieves no more than he would have obtained had he accepted the offer, he will be responsible for the costs of the party making the offer from the date of the offer or the latest date for acceptance of the offer specified in the *Calderbank* letter (usually 21 days from the date of the letter).

Part 36 offers

Parties can also make an offer pursuant to CPR Part 36, the effect of which is similar to the *Calderbank* offer.

A valid Part 36 offer must:

–   be in writing and expressly state that it is a Part 36 offer;

– state whether it relates to the whole of the claim or only certain issues, and whether it takes into account any counter-claim (ie an application for interim rent); and

– state that it remains open for 21 days and if not accepted after 21 days may only be accepted if the court gives permission or costs are agreed.

It will be treated as 'without prejudice save as to costs' and so cannot be disclosed to the trial judge until all substantive issues in the proceedings have been decided.

The recipient of a Part 36 offer can, within seven days of receipt, ask for clarification of the offer and if it is not provided voluntarily, the recipient can apply for an order for clarification.

The effect on costs

A Part 36 offer has potential cost advantages over a *Calderbank* offer for a tenant. This is because the general rule is that acceptance of a Part 36 offer will result in the defendant landlord incurring liability for the claimant tenant's costs of the proceedings. *Calderbank* letters will usually (subject to the stage of the proceedings at which they are made) suggest that the offer proposed is capable of acceptance on the basis that each side bears its own costs.

When coming to consider the effect on costs of a Part 36 offer the court will look at:

(1) the stage in the proceedings at which it was made;

(2) the information available to the parties;

(3) the conduct of the parties with regard to the provision of any further information by way of clarification; and

(4) the extent to which the offer resembles or differs from the party's open position.

Whilst the court is not bound to make a particular order as to costs because of the existence of a *Calderbank* or Part 36 offer, in practice its existence will form an integral part of a party's submission on costs.

Other consequences

The general rules on the consequences of a Part 36 offer are as follows.

(1) If a Part 36 offer made by the defendant landlord is accepted by the claimant tenant within 21 days of its receipt, in circumstances where there are not less than 21 days before trial, the tenant will be entitled to his costs of the proceedings up to the date of serving the notice of acceptance.

(2) If a Part 36 offer made by the claimant tenant is accepted by the defendant landlord within 21 days of its receipt, the tenant will be entitled to his costs of the proceedings up to the date upon which the landlord serves notice of acceptance.

Therefore, there are potential cost advantages to a tenant of the Part 36 procedure and in practice landlords will offer to settle by way of *Calderbank* letters rather than the Part 36 procedure.

If a defendant landlord makes a Part 36 offer which is not accepted and at trial the claimant tenant fails to obtain an order which improves upon the Part 36 offer, the tenant is likely to be ordered to pay the landlord's costs from the latest date upon which the Part 36 offer was capable of acceptance without the court's permission.

Similarly, if a tenant's Part 36 offer is rejected by a landlord who subsequently fails to improve upon it at trial, the landlord is likely to incur liability for the tenant's costs, at least from the latest date on which the Part 36 offer was capable of acceptance without the court's permission.

In this situation the court is also empowered to order that the landlord pay costs on an indemnity basis and to order interest on those costs at a penal rate of up to 10% above base rate.

6.10   COSTS GENERALLY

In renewal proceedings, the usual position is that no order is made as to costs so each side bears its own costs.

However, CPR Part 44 does give the court a wide discretion on costs.

The general rule remains that the unsuccessful party will be ordered to pay the costs of the litigation incurred by the successful party. It is unusual, however, in an unopposed renewal situation for either party to be wholly successful.

In deciding what order (if any) to make about costs the rules require the court to have regard to all the circumstances, including:

(1) the conduct of the parties (before as well as during the proceedings);

(2) whether a party has succeeded on part of his case, even if he has not been wholly successful; and

(3) any offer to settle.

Under CPR, r 44.3(6) the court has the power to make a variety of cost orders including an order requiring a party to pay:

(1) a proportion of another party's costs;

(2) a stated amount of another party's costs;

(3) costs from or until a certain date only; or

(4) costs relating to particular steps in the proceedings.

6.11 COURT ORDER FOR THE GRANT OF A NEW TENANCY

Section 36 of the Act requires the landlord to execute and the tenant to accept a lease in accordance with an order of the court.

If the tenant is not prepared to accept a lease on the terms ordered by the court, there is provision in s 36(2) entitling him to apply to the court within 14 days after the making of the order seeking the revocation of the order. Either party may also appeal against the order for a new tenancy.

Since 2 May 2000, CPR Part 52 has been in force and permission to appeal from a decision of a judge of the High Court or county court is always required in property cases. The Practice Direction to CPR Part 52 indicates that permission should normally be sought from the lower court at the hearing at which the decision to be appealed from is made.

The time for filing an appellant's notice is only 14 days after the decision being appealed from. There are detailed provisions as to the documents which must accompany the notice.

An appeal has the effect of continuing the tenancy until the expiration of 3 months, beginning with the date upon which the Court of Appeal finally disposes of the matter, plus a further:

– one month in the event that permission to appeal to the House of Lords is refused by the Court of Appeal; or

– 3 months if permission to appeal to the House of Lords is granted by the Court of Appeal but no appeal is lodged.

6.12 ALTERNATIVE DISPUTE RESOLUTION: PACT

The first part of the CPR makes it clear that the duty of the court to further the overriding objective by active case management includes a duty to encourage the parties to use an alternative dispute resolution procedure, if the court considers it to be appropriate, and to facilitate the use of that procedure: CPR, r 1.4(2)(e).

In the field of lease renewals, the best-known alternative dispute resolution procedure is Professional Arbitration on Court Terms (PACT).

Two fundamental points to note about PACT are:

(1) it is not available where renewal is opposed; and

(2) it is not a substitute for a tenant applying to court for a new tenancy or a landlord applying to court for an interim rent. It is a potential method of resolving disputed issues within the context of existing court proceedings.

Following the issue and service of an application for a new tenancy, the parties can obtain a consent order from the court referring issues in dispute for determination by an arbitrator or independent expert, who may be a surveyor or a solicitor.

In view of the duty on courts to encourage alternative dispute resolution, a judge is likely to agree to a request from the parties for a stay of the court proceedings to enable them to attempt to resolve their differences by using PACT. The length of stay is a matter for the individual judge and is likely to be subject to a requirement that the parties keep the court informed of the progress of PACT.

Perceived advantages of the PACT scheme are:

(1) flexibility – the parties are able to adapt the rules to their specific requirements and choose whether the appointed professional should be a surveyor or lawyer and whether he should act as an arbitrator or independent expert;

(2) speed – whilst the court process is quicker under the CPR, it should generally be possible to obtain a result from an independent third party more quickly than from the court;

(3) cost saving – whilst fees will still be payable, it is perceived that the ability to choose a procedure which is tailor-made for resolution of the particular issues in dispute will save costs by, for example, involving more stream-lining and/or informal procedures; and

(4) quality of decision – professionals have the expertise to make sound decisions on technical matters within their specialised practice area.

Chapter 7

WITHDRAWAL AND DISCONTINUANCE

7.1 GIVING UP THE PROPERTY

Whether or not a Section 25 Notice has been served, a tenant who is happy to leave on the contractual expiry date will be safe so long as he has ceased to occupy the premises for the purposes of his business by the contractual expiry date. Under the new law this is the effect of s 27(1A) introduced by the RRO, which codified the Court of Appeal decision in *Esselte AB v Pearl Assurance plc* [1997] 2 EG 124.

7.2 SECTION 27(1): PRE-EMPTION

A possibly more honourable course than simply leaving, for a tenant who has made his decision well in advance, would be to use s 27(1). This requires not less than 3 months' notice to be given that the tenant does not desire the tenancy to be continued, to expire on the contractual expiry date.

7.3 TENANT'S WITHDRAWAL PRIOR TO PROCEEDINGS

Where a Section 25 Notice has been served and the tenant is happy to leave on the date specified, he should not apply to court for a new tenancy. Where the tenant has served a Section 26 Request and then changes his mind, he should not apply to the court for a new tenancy.

7.4 SECTION 27(2): NO LONGER A QUARTER DAY NOTICE

If a Section 25 Notice has been served extending the tenancy to a date beyond the contractual expiry date, but court proceedings have not been issued, and the tenant wishes to end the tenancy after the contractual expiry date, he can serve not less than 3 months' notice in writing on the immediate landlord. Under the old law, this had to expire on a quarter day. Under the new law, it can expire on any day. Authority for this is s 27(2) of the Act. This notice procedure cannot be used if a Section 26 Request has already been served (s 26(4)).

There are no prescribed forms for either of these notices under s 27, so they should be sent in a form of a letter. A suitable format would be along the following lines:

EXAMPLE 1

'As Solicitors/Surveyors for and on behalf of your tenant [   ] we give you notice by this letter that they do not wish their tenancy of the property at [   ] to continue beyond its contractual expiry date.'

(It is probably safest not to specify the contractual expiry date, but check when it is to make sure that three months' notice is being given.)

EXAMPLE 2

'As Solicitors/Surveyors for and on behalf of your tenant [   ] we give you notice by this letter that they wish to end their tenancy of the property at [   ] on [specify date at least three months later].'

Because under the new law court applications can be made at any time up to the date specified in the Section 25 Notice or Section 26 Request, or even later if both parties have agreed in writing to an extension, tenants who decide not to renew are more likely to do so before proceedings have been issued, under the amended terms of s 27(2), and fewer tenants are likely to make their final decision after proceedings have been issued.

7.5   DISCONTINUANCE

If a tenant, having made his application for a new tenancy, decides that he has had enough and wants to get out, he can discontinue proceedings, in which event the tenancy will continue for another 3 months and then automatically end. There is no requirement for the tenant also to give notice under s 27.

Note that if the application for a new tenancy has been made so early in the game that proceedings are issued and then discontinued more than 3 months before the end of the contractual term, the tenancy will not end until the end of the contractual term.

7.6   WALKING AWAY AFTER CONTRACTUAL EXPIRY DATE – NO LONGER AN OPTION

Under the old law, it was not clear whether the courts would be willing to extend the decision in *Esselte* to allow a tenant to end his liability by vacating after the contractual expiry date (but without having issued proceedings for a new tenancy). There were arguments both for and against, outlined in the corresponding section of the second edition of this book.

The new law is crystal clear. Section 27(2), as amended by the RRO, says that a tenancy which is continuing under s 24 (ie the contractual expiry date of which has passed), 'shall not come to an end by reason only of the tenant ceasing to occupy the property comprised in the tenancy'.

The tenant would instead have to give not less than 3 months' notice in writing, as discussed in **7.4** above.

Note, however *Arundel Corporation v The Financial Trading Company Limited* (2000) unreported, the High Court held, on the evidence before it, that the tenant continued to occupy the premises in question for the purposes of its business on the contractual expiry date but that when it left a few months later returning the keys to the landlord and the landlord accepted the keys, changed the locks, changed the security system access code and requested that future demands for rates were sent to it, then a surrender had taken place by operation of law. The tenant's liabilities had ended at that point, even though the proceedings for a new tenancy had not been discontinued.

7.7   COURT PROCEDURES FOR DISCONTINUANCE

A tenant can discontinue its application for the grant of a new tenancy at any time, under CPR, r 38.2. The permission of the court is not required.

The procedure is to file a notice of discontinuance at court and serve a copy of it on every other party to the proceedings (in practice, this is likely only to be the landlord).

If the application to the court was made by the landlord, under the new law, then the tenant should inform the court that he does not want a new tenancy. The court 'shall' then dismiss the landlord's application (s 29(5), inserted by the RRO). Technically, this will not be 'discontinuance', but our comments about discontinuance below also cover this situation.

Remember these practical points

–   Discontinuance will leave the tenant responsible for the landlord's costs of proceedings although they will usually be quite low so long as only the formal steps have been taken.

–   Discontinuance will not prevent a claim for interim rent being pursued (*Artoc Bank & Trust Ltd v Prudential Assurance Co plc* (1984) 271 EG 454).

7.8 DILAPIDATIONS

It is vital to remember that neither withdrawal nor discontinuance will prevent the landlord pursuing any claim for dilapidations which he might have. See Chapter 9. If proceedings are to be withdrawn as part of an overall settlement with a Consent Order, the parties should always consider how dilapidations are to be dealt with, and include what they agree in the Consent Order.

Chapter 8

INTERIM RENT

8.1 INTRODUCTION

Even after an application for a new tenancy is made, the tenant remains in occupation on the same terms and conditions as before and continues to pay rent at the old rate until a new lease is agreed or ordered by the court. Before the Law of Property Act 1969 incorporated s 24A into the Act, it was in the tenant's interest to drag out negotiations and/or the court application because the court could not backdate the new rent. Section 24A of the Act introduced the concept of 'interim rent'; the landlord was allowed an increased interim rent by making application to the court. Such rent was payable from the date of issue of the landlord's application or the termination date specified in the Section 25 Notice or Section 26 Request, whichever was the later (*Stream Properties v Davies* (1972) 222 EG 1203). Consequently, once the interim rent application was issued and served, the landlord was protected.

The RRO deleted the old s 24A and replaced it with new ss 24A, 24B 24C and 24D. The main changes were:

- Where the old law applies, it is only the landlord who can apply for interim rent. Where the new law applies, either the landlord or the tenant can apply for interim rent.

- Where the old law applies, as stated above, interim rent is payable from the date of issue of the landlord's application for interim rent or the specified termination date whichever is the later. Where the new law applies, interim rent is to be payable from the earliest termination date that could have been specified in the Section 25 Notice or the earliest date which could have been specified as the commencement date for the new tenancy in the Section 26 Request.

- The principles of calculation under the old law and the new law are different.

This is an area in which it is particularly important to be aware of both the old law and the new law. So long as the renewal process began with a Section 25 Notice or a Section 26 Request on or before 31 May 2004, the old law will apply. It will be a long time before all such renewals are settled.

See Chapter 6 for the procedures for applying to court for an interim rent.

If the parties cannot agree the interim rent or the new lease is not granted for any reason, the matter will be determined by the court.

8.2 OLD LAW: FROM WHEN DOES INTERIM RENT RUN?

Where the old law applies, as stated above, it is only the landlord who can apply for interim rent. Once the landlord has applied, interim rent is payable from the date of issue of the landlord's application for interim rent or the termination date specified in the Section 25 Notice or Section 26 Request, whichever is the later.

Note that issue and service of the interim rent application are vital; in the case of *R v Gravesend County Court ex parte Patchett* [1993] 26 EG 123 the court failed to issue the landlord's application when it was first received and then attempted to backdate it to the date of receipt. When the tenant applied for judicial review, the High Court held that the county court did not have authority to issue the application retrospectively. The landlord was not represented in the case, and therefore the case does not give any guidance on whether a landlord would be entitled to compensation for what appears to be obvious maladministration by the court. The moral is for the landlord to make sure that the application has been issued.

8.3 NEW LAW: FROM WHEN DOES INTERIM RENT RUN?

Under the new law, as stated above, it is either the landlord or the tenant who can apply for interim rent.

The date from which interim rent runs is not linked to the date of the application. Instead, by the new s 24B, it is payable from the earliest date of termination that could have been specified in the landlord's Section 25 Notice or the earliest date for the commencement of the new tenancy which could have been specified in the tenant's Section 26 Request.

Where the Section 25 Notice or the Section 26 Request is served more than 6 months before the end of the contractual term, the date from which interim rent will run – if applied for – will obviously be the expiry of the contractual term.

Where the Section 25 Request or the Section 26 Notice was not served until there were less than 6 months to go before the end of the contractual term, so that the specified termination/commencement date has to be later than the end of the contractual term, the position is not entirely clear. Some commentators have assumed that interim rent would still be payable from the expiry of the contractual term. The writers believe that the new s 26B is more likely to be interpreted as providing for the interim rent to commence on the earliest date of termination/commencement which could have been specified in *the actual* Section 25 Notice or Section 26 Request; in other words, 6 months after *the actual* Section 25 Notice or Section 26 Request.

This change in the law changes some of the tactics which have become traditional:

– Where the market has fallen and the property is over-rented, a landlord can no longer retain the old rent by not applying for an interim rent. The tenant can apply.

– Equally, in a rising market where the landlord has not served a Section 25 Notice ending the lease on the contractual expiry date, the tenant cannot fend off the interim rent by making a Section 26 Request for a new tenancy to begin, say, 364 days into the future. Once an application has been made for interim rent (which in this case would surely be by the landlord), it will be payable from the earliest date which the tenant *could* have specified in his Section 26 Request.

Remember always that interim rent still has to be applied for. If neither party has bothered to apply, the court cannot award it!

Note also there is a new time limit for applications in the new s 24A(3). The application, by either party, must be made no less than six months after the termination of the relevant tenancy.

8.4   OLD LAW: PRINCIPLES OF CALCULATION

Where the old law applies, the interim rent is to be based on the principles set out in s 34 of the Act (see **5.5**), valuing the property demised by the old lease on the terms of the old lease but based on a yearly tenancy. The lack of security for the tenant in a yearly tenancy has traditionally been seen to allow a discount.

By s 24A(3) of the Act, the court must 'have regard to' the old rent. This has been interpreted as allowing a 'cushion' between the old rent and the market rent, an expression used in *English Exporters (London) Ltd v Eldonwall Ltd* (1973) 225 EG 433 and in *Charles Follett Ltd v Cabtell Investment Co Ltd* (1987) 283 EG 195. The correct procedure is for the court to assess the rent which would be payable on the basis of s 34, apply any discount for a yearly tenancy (thus creating the 'interim market rent') and then 'having regard to' the old rent to assess any further discount: *French v Commercial Union* [1993] 24 EG 115.

Examples of discounts

Each case will depend on the evidence given and the extent of the difference between the old rent and the new rent. Some leading examples of discounts are as follows.

(1) *English Exporters (London) Ltd v Eldonwall Ltd* (1973) 225 EG 433
     –   old rent £7,655 pa

- new rent £16,000 pa
- 6.25% discount for yearly tenancy and further 6.66% discount for 'having regard' – total discount 12.5%.

(2) *Janes (Gowns) Ltd v Harlow Development Corporation* (1979) 253 EG 799
- old rent £2,100 pa
- new rent £12,500 pa
- 10% discount for yearly tenancy and further 10% for 'having regard' – total discount 18%.

(3) *Ratners (Jewellers) Limited v Lemnoll* (1980) 255 EG 987
- old rent £11,250 pa
- new rent £23,038 pa
- 15% discount for yearly tenancy and further 10.6% for 'having regard' – total discount 24%.

(4) *Charles Follett Ltd v Cabtell Investment Co Ltd* (1987) 283 EG 195
- old rent £13,500 pa
- new rent £106,000 pa
- 24.5% discount for yearly tenancy and further 50% discount for 'having regard' – total discount 62.3%.

(5) In *Conway v Arthur* [1988] 40 EG 120, a 15% discount was held on appeal to have been too low. A new trial was ordered.

(6) *French v Commercial Union* [1993] 24 EG 115
- old rent £10,475 pa
- new rent £31,858 pa
- 10% discount for yearly tenancy (agreed between the parties) and further 10% discount for 'having regard'; however, these discounts are taken from the value of the property when interim rent became payable on 2 March 1987, whereas the new rent was calculated on the basis of November 1991.

County court cases

Some county court cases (which, of course, are not in any sense precedents, even in other county courts) have produced the following discounts.

(1) *Boots The Chemists Ltd v Pinkland Ltd* and *Thorn EMI Plc v Pinkland Ltd* [1992] 28 EG 118. The report simply quotes the rent in terms of square footage without giving the number of square feet, so it is not possible to compare the old and new rents, but states that there was a 5% discount for a yearly tenancy and a further 10% for 'having regard'.

(2) *Department of the Environment v Allied Freehold Property Trust Ltd* [1992] 45 EG 156. The old rent was £1,150, fixed in 1949. The new rent is not set out in the report. The court awarded an interim rent of £70,400 which included a

12½% deduction for a yearly tenancy, but declined to give any discount for 'having regard' because of the benefit the tenant had already had of a low rent in inflationary times.

(3) Contrast *Blythwood Plant Hire Ltd v Spiers Ltd (in receivership)* [1992] 48 EG 117. The old rent is not stated in the report, but as the tenant had been holding over since July 1946 it can be assumed to have been very low. The new rent awarded was £41,700 with an interim rent (payable from March 1991) of £20,000 – a total discount of 52% which is not sub-divided.

(4) Contrast also *Amarjee v Barrowfen Properties Ltd* [1993] 30 EG 98, in which the Wood Green County Court simply accepted the landlord's expert's view that the conventional figure for interim rent was the new rent less 10% without attempting to divide it between a discount for a yearly tenancy and 'having regard'.

8.5 WILL AN INTERIM RENT UNDER THE OLD LAW ALWAYS BE BELOW THE NEW RENT?

There is no reason in principle why an interim rent calculated under the old law should not, in a falling market, be equal to or higher than the rent calculated under s 34 for the new tenancy. The authors are not aware of any reported case where this has happened.

Interim rent calculated under the old law is based on valuations current on the date from which it is payable, which may be some years earlier than the valuation date for the new lease. A good example is *French v Commercial Union* when the valuation date for interim rent was more than 4 years before the hearing in the Court of Appeal, but note that in that case the market had risen during this period. Remember also that interim rent is assessed under the old law on the basis of the terms of the old lease, albeit a yearly tenancy. The parties may agree an updated (ie more onerous) new lease but be unable to agree an interim rent.

It is difficult to speculate on the principles the court would use, but presumably if the interim market rent was higher than the passing rent under the continuing tenancy (because the market had risen before the valuation date and fallen thereafter) there would still be scope to include a cushion.

8.6 OLD LAW: DOES A LANDLORD REALLY WANT TO APPLY FOR AN INTERIM RENT?

It has traditionally been assumed that an interim rent calculated under the old law would always be higher than the passing rent at the end of the contractual term, which would normally have been based on market rents at least 5 years earlier. That would not necessarily be correct in a market which had fallen for some time. This is an issue which will continue even after such a market turns and resumes its rise, as the valuation date for the purpose of calculating interim rent is the date from which it will become payable.

If the expiring lease contains a last day rent review, the rent payable while the tenant is holding over will be the market rent at the end of the old term, which is very likely to be higher than an interim rent. A landlord with the benefit of this will be unlikely to apply for an interim rent.

If the rent payable under the new lease were less than the rent payable under the old lease during the continuation tenancy, a landlord would wish to delay proceedings as long as possible and therefore would have no reason to induce the tenant to believe his interests would be prejudiced by delay by applying for and pursuing an application for interim rent.

A landlord who has not obtained full valuation advice before the contractual expiry date should nevertheless apply for interim rent as a protective measure, being ready to withdraw the application if evidence indicates that an interim rent would be lower than the contractual passing rent. The Civil Procedure Rules allow a landlord to withdraw an application for interim rent as of right, although at the risk of having to pay the tenant's costs incurred in connection with that application.

Another possible option for a landlord would be to apply to the court to fix an interim rent of a specified figure, thereafter arguing that the court had jurisdiction only to accept or reject that figure but not to substitute another. The authors have seen an application made in these terms but are not aware of any such application being taken to trial. A tenant would presumably use the objection that s 24A(1) of the Act allows a landlord to apply to the court to determine the rent which it would be reasonable for the tenant to pay and that an application limited to a specified figure would either be invalid or trigger this general jurisdiction.

8.7 NEW LAW: PRINCIPLES OF CALCULATION

Where the new law applies, the interim rent is to be calculated on the basis of the new s 24C and s 24D.

The new s 24C applies where the landlord did not object to the grant of a new tenancy and a new tenancy is granted of the whole of the property comprised in the old tenancy.

This will surely cover most lease renewals.

In principle, in such cases the 'rent payable under and at the commencement of the new tenancy shall also be the interim rent' (s 24C(2)). In other words, the 'cushion' which applies under the old law has been removed. It follows that in a rising market a tenant will no longer gain a financial benefit by stringing out negotiations and proceedings; the interim rent will be no lower than the rent under the new lease.

Note that an interim rent awarded on this basis will effectively have been calculated on the basis of market conditions just before the new lease starts. This is because the new rent will either have been agreed between the parties, on the basis of their understanding of current market conditions, or awarded by the court under s 34, on the basis of the evidence of current market conditions provided to the court.

However, there are statutory exceptions to the general rule. They are so wide that many argue they will apply more often than the general rule will apply.

Where the landlord or the tenant satisfies the court that the rent payable under and at the commencement of the new tenancy 'differs substantially from' what is defined as 'the relevant rent', namely the rent which the court would have fixed under s 34 if the new tenancy has commenced on the date from which interim rent is payable, then the interim rent will be 'the relevant rent', not the rent under the new lease.

The test here is that the market must have changed, either up or down, to an extent which has a 'substantial' effect on rental value. Obviously, this can happen:

– over a short period, if the market is moving fast;

– over a long period if the market is moving consistently in one direction.

In practice, where this exception applies there will be a 'cushion' between the old rent and the new rent. However, this will be different from the 'cushion' which applies under the old law:

– The interim rent will be based on the terms of the new lease, not (as under the old law) on the terms of the old lease.

– The interim rent will not be on the basis of a yearly tenancy.

– The court will not be required to 'have regard to' the old rent.

It follows that the cases decided under the old law should not be relevant where this exception applies. The court will simply apply the statutory criteria in s 34 at the date from which interim rent became payable, and the parties will seek to negotiate an interim rent knowing that this is what the court would do.

There is a second, and even more complicated, exception.

This applies where the landlord or the tenant satisfies the court that the terms of the new tenancy differ from the terms of the old tenancy to such an extent that the rent payable under the new lease is substantially different from the rent which would have been determined under s 34 to be payable under a tenancy which commenced on the same day as the new tenancy and whose other terms were the same as the old lease.

The first exception depends on the extent to which the market has moved. The second exception depends on the extent to which the terms of the lease have changed.

Where the second exception applies (whether or not the first exception also applies) the interim rent is defined by new s 24C(6) as 'the rent which it is reasonable for the tenant to pay' while the old lease continues and the court must have regard to:

– the rent payable under the terms of the old lease; and

– the rent payable under any sub-tenancy of part of the property comprised in the old lease.

However, subject to that, subsections 34(1) and (2) are to apply as they would apply if a new tenancy of the whole of the property comprised in the old tenancy was granted by the court for a term equal to the term of the new tenancy which has actually been granted.

We can only speculate how this test will be applied. The invitation to the court to have regard to the old rent suggests that there will be discounts similar to those which cases under the old law allowed for 'having regard'. However:

– there will not be an additional discount on the basis of a yearly tenancy; and

– rents receivable under sub-tenancies of part will also be relevant.

Obviously, very few renewal leases are granted on terms absolutely identical to the old lease. The extent to which changes in the terms have a 'substantial' effect on rental value will ultimately be a question for the court which they will have to decide on the basis of expert valuation evidence. Where the old lease was relatively up-to-date, so that evidence of lettings on comparable terms are available in the market, the expert valuers will have evidence to produce. Their task will be more difficult where the old lease was in terms which would now be considered obsolete, as many expiring leases originally granted for 25 years or more will be. Obviously, substantial updating (or complete re-writing) will have an effect on rental value, but it may not be easy to prove how much of an effect.

All the comments above apply where the landlord did not object to renewal and the new lease was granted. The new s 24D covers other cases. The most obvious other cases will be:

–   where the landlord originally objected to renewal, but either withdrew his objection or fought and lost;

–   where the landlord originally objected to renewal and won, but interim rent was applied for and the tenant remained in occupation after the date from which it was payable;

–   where the landlord did not object to renewal but the tenant decided not to renew, interim rent was applied for and the tenant remained in occupation after the date from which interim rent was payable.

In these cases, yet another set of criteria will apply.

Under s 24D, the interim rent in these cases is 'the rent which it is reasonable for the tenant to pay' while the old lease continues having regard to:

–   the rent payable under the terms of the old lease; and

–   the rent payable under any underleases of part of the property comprised in the old lease

but on the basis of a yearly tenancy.

This looks pretty similar to principles of calculation under the old law, save that the court must also have regard to the rent payable under underleases of part. Most renewals will not have underleases of part.

8.8   NEW LAW: ARE LAST DAY RENT REVIEWS A DEAD LETTER?

Where old law applies, the benefit to the landlord of a last day rent review was that the contractual rent following the expiry of the contractual term would be no lower than the market rent at that time (as distinct from no lower than the market rent at the previous review, probably 5 years earlier). The landlord could preserve that market rent during negotiations for a new lease by the simple expedient of not applying for interim rent.

The potential unfairness of this is why most tenants' solicitors have in recent years strongly resisted the inclusion of last day rent reviews. Whether they succeed depends, of course, on the bargaining strength of the parties at the time the lease is granted.

Where the new law applies, the tenant can trump the landlord's last day rent review by applying for interim rent itself.

Does this mean (as one of the writers once argued at a seminar) that the last day rent review is a dead letter under the new law? Not necessarily. Even though the tenant can now apply for interim rent itself, there will always be somebody, somewhere who forgets to instruct their solicitors to do so, and some solicitors, somewhere, who fail to do so.

8.9   ADVICE FOR LANDLORDS

Once the landlord has decided to seek an interim rent, he might consider the following.

(1) Where the old law applies he should make sure an application is made before the termination date. Where the new law applies, he must make sure the application is made no later than 6 months after the termination of the old tenancy (s 24A(3)).

(2) If the tenant is seeking to remain in occupation for as long as possible, he should use this as a bargaining tool by threatening to have it determined by the court as a separate issue. However, the costs of obtaining evidence should be borne in mind.

(3) Once the application has been made, the landlord can accept rent at the old rate whilst the tenancy continues by virtue of s 24 without being taken to have agreed the old level of rent as the rent for the new tenancy.

(4) If disputing the validity of the tenant's counter notice (where the old law applies) or application (in any case), the landlord should still apply for interim rent in case it is valid, but do so specifically without prejudice to those objections.

(5) See **2.8** for a particular problem with interim rent when there is a chain of tenancies.

(6) Where a tenant who is not the original tenant withdraws from renewal proceedings because he cannot afford the market rent and/or he is insolvent, and the interim rent which would be awarded is higher than the passing rent under the expired lease, a landlord's first response is likely to be to cut his losses by obtaining an interim rent award and then recovering it from previous tenants. The landlord must consider carefully whether an interim rent will be recoverable before incurring the expenses of obtaining an award. An original tenant with continuing liability (ie: under

an 'old lease' for the purposes of the Landlord and Tenant (Covenants) Act 1995) who has assigned his interest will not be liable following the expiry of the contractual term unless the lease specifically so states, and any express continuation of liability will be limited to the contractual rent unless it specifically includes liability for an interim rent awarded under s 24A of the Act (*City of London Corporation v Fell; Herbert Duncan Ltd v Cluttons* [1993] 4 EG 115). The same principles would surely apply to the interpretation of licences to assign where there have been intermediate assignees with continuing liability.

(7) Note the possible application of s 42(2)(c) of the Act, which provides that an assignment of a tenancy from one member of a group of companies to another shall not be treated as a change in the person of the tenant possibly extending the liability of the assignor group company on the basis that no assignment is deemed to have taken place. This possibility was specifically referred to by one member of the Court of Appeal in *City of London Corporation v Fell*, but that case did not concern group companies and the opinion seems inconsistent with the tone of the Court of Appeal's decision.

Where the old law applies, only a landlord can apply for interim rent. If he chooses not to do so, a tenant cannot himself apply. Therefore a tenant who believes that the market rent is less than the passing rent under the continuing tenancy has all the more incentive to expedite the proceedings and achieve a new lease as swiftly as possible.

Where the new law applies, either the landlord or the tenant can apply for interim rent. Therefore, a tenant who believes that the market rent is less than the passing rate under the continuing tenancy will want to make sure they take advantage of their new rights and apply for an interim rent!

Chapter 9

DILAPIDATIONS

9.1   CLAIMS FOR DILAPIDATIONS

All leases have some sort of repairing covenant and therefore in all renewals there is a possibility that the landlord may have a claim for dilapidations under the old lease.

Even if the lease is to be renewed, the landlord can still serve a Schedule of Dilapidations and a Section 146 Notice requiring the work to be carried out within a reasonable time, or monetary compensation to be paid. The tenant will seek to establish that some items on the Schedule are either incorrect or unnecessary and that the monetary compensation to which the landlord is entitled should be restricted to the reduction in the value of his reversion, under s 18 of the Landlord and Tenant Act 1927.

As an alternative, if the lease is to be renewed, the landlord will argue that the repairing obligation should be to 'put and keep' the premises in good repair. This is on the basis that any disrepair at the commencement of the new lease will have arisen because the tenant has failed to comply with his repairing covenants in the old lease. The advantage of this is that it does not require a formal Schedule of Dilapidations to be drawn up.

A more detailed alternative is for a Schedule to be drawn up and for the new lease to contain a specific covenant to carry out the works in that Schedule within a specified period of time. On that basis the repairing obligation need not be 'put and keep' but can be the more usual 'keep in repair'.

9.2   REDEVELOPMENT AND CLAIMS FOR DILAPIDATIONS

Where a landlord objects to renewal on the grounds of intended redevelopment the tenant will argue against any claim for dilapidations that the property is to be redeveloped and therefore there has been no reduction in the value of the reversion.

9.3   THE SERVICE CHARGE TRAP

An intermediate tenant with a full repairing lease who has sub-let the whole of his demise in parts, on a service charge basis, and whose tenancy will therefore terminate on the contractual expiry date, must avoid the service charge trap. The landlord may serve a Schedule of Dilapidations and claim damages if the works are not done. He will only be able to serve Schedules of Dilapidations on his tenants in respect of their individual demises and those tenants will argue that the intermediate reversion was worthless whatever the state of the property. Worse, the intermediate tenant will only be able to recover the cost of repairing any common parts through the service charge if the work is actually carried out before the intermediate lease ends. Note, however, that where a landlord charges a service charge to an intermediate tenant which the intermediate tenant recovers in turn from a sub-tenant, the intermediate tenant will be able to recover from the sub-tenant service charges which were incurred before the intermediate lease expired, even after its expiry: *Electricity Supply Nominees Ltd v Thorn EMI Retail (1991) Ltd* [1991] 35 EG 114.

9.4   FORFEITURE ON GROUNDS OF DISREPAIR

When dealing with lease renewals, it is important to remember that the protection normally afforded by the Leasehold Property (Repairs) Act 1938 will not apply (because the lease will have less than 3 years unexpired) and therefore the landlord will be able to forfeit the lease on grounds of disrepair, following service of a Section 146 Notice, without first obtaining the consent of the court. To protect his position, the tenant must apply to the court for relief from forfeiture as soon as a Section 146 Notice is received.

Chapter 10

COMPENSATION

10.1 INTRODUCTION

The tenant is entitled to compensation on quitting the premises where his right to a new lease is lost through the landlord proving grounds (e), (f) or (g) of s 30(1). The compensation provisions are set out in s 37 of the Act.

Where the only grounds of opposition are one or more of those three, the tenant can claim compensation even if he makes no application for a new tenancy to the court, or if he does apply and then discontinues (now s 37(1C)), or if the landlord withdraws the ground but the tenant leaves anyway (the last point was established in *Lloyds Bank Ltd v City of London Corporation* [1983] 1 All ER 92). A Section 26 Request made by a tenant that had already committed itself to taking other premises, to which the landlord responded by serving a counter notice objecting to renewal on ground (f), was enough to trigger compensation: *Sun Life Assurance plc v Thales Tracs Limited and another* [2001] 2 EGLR 57. The tenant's state of mind when the Section 26 Request was served was legally irrelevant.

If the landlord combines one or more of grounds (a) to (d) with (e), (f) or (g), compensation is only available if the court specifies grounds (e), (f) or (g) as the ground or grounds on which a new lease has been refused. Note that this cannot happen unless an application is made for a new tenancy and pursued to trial. A landlord who can establish a case under grounds (e), (f) or (g) but could also establish a case under one or more of grounds (a) to (d) will gain a tactical advantage by including that ground also; the tenant may be unwilling to incur the time and expense of a full trial.

10.2 BASIS OF CALCULATION

To calculate the level of compensation, take the rateable value of the premises at the date of giving the Section 25 Notice or the landlord's counter notice after the tenant's Section 26 Request (*Plessey & Co v Eagle Pensions Fund Ltd* [1990] 35 EG 52) and multiply by the appropriate multiplier.

The present form of the appropriate multiplier is set out in the Landlord and Tenant Act 1954 (Appropriate Multiplier) Order 1990 and is as follows.

(1) If the date of giving the Section 25 Notice or Section 26 Counter Notice was before 1 April 1990, the tenant will be entitled to three times the old rateable value of the premises.

(2) If the date of giving the Section 25 Notice or Section 26 Counter Notice was after 31 March 1990, the tenant will be entitled to a sum equal to the rateable value of the premises.

The date to which the tenant's period of occupation of the premises is calculated is the date on which the tenant leaves the premises (*Cardshops v John Lewis Properties* (1982) 263 EG 791).

In either of the above cases, the appropriate multiplier is doubled where the tenant (or his predecessors in the same business) has occupied the premises for more than 14 years. See Figure 3 below.

To satisfy the 14-year requirement the tenant can aggregate periods of occupation of successors in business. The 14-year period of occupation has to be satisfied up to the termination date specified in the Section 25 Notice or the Section 26 Request, even if this is later than the contractual expiry date and the tenancy ended on the contractual expiry date as a result: *Esselte AB v Pearl Assurance plc* [1997] 2 EG 124; *Sight & Sound Education Ltd v Books etc Ltd* [1999] 3 EGLR 45. The de minimis rule does not apply (*Department of Environment v Royal Insurance* (1986) 282 EG 208 – 13 years and 363 days was not enough for the higher multiplier).

On the other hand, the Court of Appeal has held that whenever business premises are empty for only a short period, whether mid-term or before or after trading at either end of the lease, it should not be held that business occupancy has ceased (or not started) for that period so long as during the period there exists no rival for the role of business occupant and that the premises are not being used for some other, non-business purpose: *Bacchiocchi v Academic Agency Limited* [1998] 3 EGLR 157; and that the tenant may include time while it was prevented by circumstances beyond its control from being in occupation, for example because of a fire: *Morrison Holdings v Manders* [1976] 2 All ER 205.

It is not easy to reconcile these cases. In *Bacchiocchi*, leaving the property empty for 10 days was not long enough to lead to the conclusion that business occupancy had ceased. In *Sight & Sound Education Ltd*, the tenant vacated before 28 September and the continuation tenancy ended on 25 February of the following year and that was long enough to defeat any argument that occupation had continued until the later date. It is all a question of time, and no firm dividing line has yet been drawn.

The RRO introduced a new s 37(3A) into the Act. Where the new law applies (ie the Section 25 Notice or the Section 26 Request was dated on or after 1 June 2004), if the 14-year requirement is satisfied in relation to part of the holding

Figure 3: Compensation payable

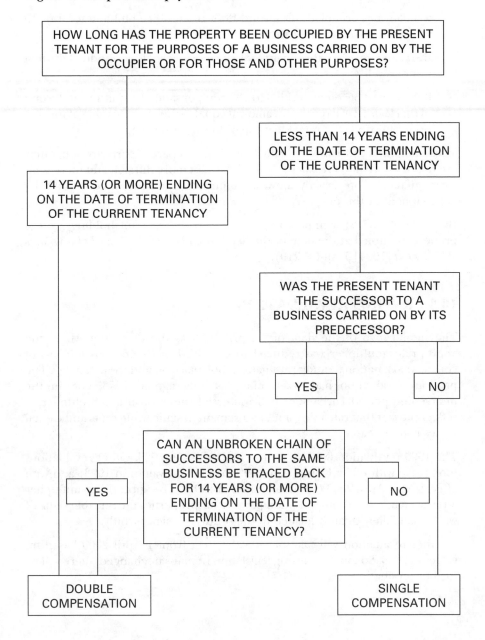

but not in relation to the rest of it, compensation is calculated separately for each part and the tenant receives the aggregate. For example:

–   a tenant has occupied the second floor of an office building for, say, 15 years, under successive leases;

–   five years ago, when the tenant took the most recent lease, it added the first floor as well;

–   if the tenant becomes entitled to s 37 compensation on quitting at the end of that lease, it will receive an amount equal to the rateable value of the first floor plus twice the rateable value of the second floor.

These amounts can easily be calculated if the separate parts are separately rated. If they are not, the calculation will be a lot more difficult and there is no clear guidance on exactly how a composite rateable value should be apportioned for this purpose.

By virtue of s 37(2), compensation applies to the relevant holding, ie, the property occupied at the date of the Section 25 Notice (*Edicron Ltd v William Whiteley Ltd* [1984] 1 All ER 219).

10.3   RATING REVALUATION

The significance of the date of 1 April 1990 as the date after which the appropriate multiplier was reduced to one-third of its previous level is, of course, that a national rating revaluation took place on and from that day. The previous revaluation had taken place as long ago as 1973, and in the intervening period Parliament had increased the appropriate multiplier to reflect the fact that rateable values had remained static while rents and capital values had increased.

The 1990 revaluation was based on rental values in 1988. Other revaluations took place with effect from 1 April 1995 (based on values in 1993) and with effect from 1 April 2000 (based on values in 1998). The appropriate multiplier was not changed, so compensation payable for properties the rateable value of which had fallen (mainly located in the south) fell significantly.

Another revaluation will take place with effect from 1 April 2005 based on values in 2003. So long as existing legislation remains unchanged, there will be further revaluations every 5 years.

10.4 TAX

Compensation paid under s 37 is normally free of capital gains tax as it does not give rise to a gain (*Drummond (Inspector of Taxes) v Austin Brown* [1984] 3 WLR 381).

Compensation under s 37 is not consideration for a surrender and does not bear VAT.

If the tenant agrees to surrender the lease in return for an amount equal to the statutory compensation, the amount will bear VAT and will be taken into account for capital gains tax. The landlord will have to pay stamp duty land tax on the compensation as consideration for a surrender.

10.5 COMPENSATION FOR MISREPRESENTATION

If the court is induced not to grant a new lease by misrepresentation, or the concealment of material facts, the court has the power to order the landlord to pay the tenant 'such sum as appears sufficient' as compensation for damage or loss sustained by the tenant as a result. This is now s 37A(1).

Where the tenant leaves, either after making but then discontinuing an application for a new tenancy or without making such an application at all and it appears to the court that the tenant did so because of misrepresentation or the concealment of material facts, then the court may order the landlord to pay the tenant 'such sum as appears sufficient as compensation for damage or loss sustained by the tenant as a result of quitting the holding'. This is s 37A(2).

These provisions are separate from, and additional to, the provisions for statutory compensation in s 37 itself. Landlords who have to pay compensation under s 37A will surely argue that the court should take into account compensation to which the tenant would be entitled under s 37 (which, because it is based on rateable value, not on loss, may in some cases be greater than the tenant's loss). Bearing in mind that the court will be ordering compensation because it and/or the tenant has been misled, the court may well try to find a basis for not requiring the tenant to set off its statutory compensation.

10.6 CONTRACTING OUT

It is possible for the landlord and the tenant to contract out of compensation provisions or restrict the amount payable, but by s 38(2) such an agreement is only valid where the premises have not been occupied for business purposes by the tenant (or predecessors in the same business) for 5 years or more preceding the date on which the tenant is to quit. The agreement would be valid if there had been a change of occupier, and the occupiers had not carried on the same business during this 5-year period.

Note that the period of 5 years or more must be a period of occupation under a tenancy protected by the Act. This is illustrated by *London Baggage Co (Charing Cross) Ltd v Railtrack plc (No 2)* [2003] 1 EGLR 141 in which the tenant had lost its renewal rights (by failing to serve a counter notice in time) but had remained in occupation of the premises after the termination of its tenancy as a tenant at will. The lease contained a clause denying the tenant compensation. The tenant had occupied for some 4 years under the protection of the Act and then for some 20 months as a tenant at will; only the first period counted, the clause was effective and no compensation was payable.

At the beginning of the tenancy granted to a tenant who is to begin a new business in the property it will not be known whether an agreement excluding the right to compensation will be effective by the time that the tenant quits. Nevertheless, the landlord's solicitor should if possible seek to exclude that right in a lease for a term exceeding 5 years in case there is a change in both the occupier and the business carried on during the last 5 years.

Chapter 11

IMPROVEMENTS: SOME COMMENTS ON THE LANDLORD AND TENANT ACT 1927

11.1 TENANT'S RIGHTS TO CARRY OUT IMPROVEMENTS

Part I of the Landlord and Tenant Act 1927 allows tenants under business leases to carry out improvements to their holdings and entitles them to compensation for those improvements (subject to conditions) when the leases end.

The property must be used wholly or partly for a trade or business.

11.2 THE STATUTORY PROCEDURE

The tenant must give to his landlord notice of his intention to carry out improvements together with specifications and plans. That notice must be in writing, but there is no prescribed form. On receipt of this the landlord may give a notice of objection within a 3-month period. Again, there is no prescribed form. Alternatively, the landlord may within a 2-month period offer to carry out the improvements in consideration of a reasonable increase of rent or of such increase of rent as the tribunal (ie the High Court or the county court) may determine.

On receipt of a notice of objection the tenant may apply to the court and if the court is satisfied that the improvement:

(1) is of such a nature as to be calculated to add to the letting value of the holding at the termination of the tenancy; and

(2) is reasonable and suitable to the character of the holding; and

(3) will not diminish the value of any other property belonging to the same landlord or to any superior landlord from whom the immediate landlord of the tenant directly or indirectly holds,

then the court may certify that the improvement is proper, and the tenant can carry out the improvement notwithstanding any contrary provision in the lease, even if the lease contains an absolute prohibition against that work. Note that no certificate can be granted if the improvements have been completed before the date of the trial (*Hogarth Health Club v Westbourne Investments Ltd* [1990] 1 EGCR 89).

The tenant can require the landlord to provide a certificate that the work has been duly executed. If the landlord fails to do so within one month, the tenant may apply to the court for a certificate.

Where the landlord has offered to carry out the improvements and the tenant has accepted the offer, the landlord will be bound by such undertaking, so if he fails to comply with it the tenant will have the remedy against him of damages and specific performance.

11.3   COMPENSATION FOR IMPROVEMENTS

If he makes the necessary application within the time-limits referred to in **3.6** and does not renew his tenancy under the 1954 Act, the tenant is entitled at the end of the lease to compensation for an improvement which increases the letting value of the property unless:

–   the improvement was made before 1927; or

–   the tenant was obliged under a contract for valuable consideration, including a building lease, to make the improvement.

Compensation for improvements under the 1927 Act must not exceed:

–   the net addition to the value of the property as a direct result of the improvement; or

–   the reasonable cost of carrying out the improvement at the termination of the tenancy, less an amount equal to any cost of putting the works constituting the improvement into a reasonable state of repair (save to the extent that such costs are covered by the liability of the tenant under any repairing covenant).

In calculating such compensation, regard is also to be had to the intended future use of the property and to any intention to demolish it, or to make structural alterations to it.

Chapter 12

THE TELECOMMUNICATIONS CODE

12.1 INTRODUCTION

One industry that in recent years has been especially concerned by the issue of continuation of occupation, although not by a renewal of tenancy *per se*, is the telecommunications business. Indeed, a code has been established specially to meet the very individual needs of the industry. The Telecommunications Code ('the Code') is contained within Sch 2 to the Telecommunications Act 1984. However, the term 'Code' is somewhat misleading because it has connotations of a voluntary code adopted by suppliers in order to improve consumers' rights. Any apparent similarity between the procedures of the Code and those of the (1954) Act is also misleading.

The fundamental point about the Code, where it applies, is that in terms of ultimate control of the property in question, it is likely to achieve completely the opposite result from the Act. In essence, under the Act, although tenants are granted substantial protection rights, a landlord which wants the property back for development or for its own use can be reasonably assured of achieving this, subject to the payment of compensation. By contrast, where the Code applies to an agreement, the landowner has no such control and permanent rights can be created, subject only to a right to compensation, the quantum of which is likely to be heavily disputed.

The reality is that the Code has introduced compulsory purchase powers for the licensed operators thinly disguised under the Code concept. Although as a matter of commercial practice the operators prefer to obtain rights by voluntary agreement, it can only be a matter of time before an increasingly competitive market, spurred on by the ever-accelerating technical advances in the telecommunications field, induces some of them to use their compulsory purchase powers either indirectly in terms of improving their negotiating position, or directly by invoking the procedures under the Code. The process is likely to gain further momentum in respect of commercial premises in the light of the increasing popular resistance to equipment being located in residential areas due to concerns over potential health risks.

12.2 CONDITIONS WHEN THE CODE APPLIES

The operator (which in this case may be a variety of telecommunications companies such as Vodafone, Orange or One to One) must have a licence granted under the provisions of the Telecommunications Act 1984. The licence will normally state expressly that the Code applies.

The apparatus to be installed must be listed in the operator's licence. Any equipment which is not listed in the licence will not be covered by the provisions of the Code. As is seen below, this will have an impact on the rights that the occupier or landlord can enforce against the operator.

Finally and perhaps most significantly, there has to be a written agreement with the occupier of the land in question (paragraph 2) or, in the absence of a written agreement, a court order under paragraph 5 (see below). The occupier need not necessarily be the owner but may be a licensee or tenant.

In essence, once the statutory powers are effective they can bind:

(1) any party who granted the right;

(2) any party who agreed to the right being granted;

(3) any third party who has an interest in the land despite the fact that it has not given its consent to an agreement with the operator or agreed to the grant of the right.

It follows that a tenant as occupier of the land can enter into an agreement with an operator which will bind the landlord even if the landlord has not consented to it. The only consolation for the landlord is that the operator can rely on the rights granted by the occupier only for as long as the occupier remains in possession of the land. After the occupier has surrendered possession of the land, the landlord is no longer bound and can take steps to recover the property. (This is discussed in more detail at **12.4**.)

12.3 RIGHTS UNDER THE CODE

Paragraph 2

If the provisions of the Code apply, the operator is automatically entitled to the following rights:

(1) to execute any works on the land for or in connection with the installation, maintenance, adjustment, repair or alteration of apparatus;

(2) to keep the apparatus installed on, under or over the land; and

(3) to enter the land to inspect any apparatus kept or installed on, under or over the land for the purposes of the operator's system.

Paragraph 5

Paragraph 5 of the Code provides an attractive alternative for the operator. If the occupier does not enter into a contract with the operator, the operator can give notice to the occupier setting out the terms which it requires.

After a notice period of 28 days, the operator can apply to the court for an order granting the rights it requests, thus dispensing with the need for an agreement. The court can make the order, but only so long as:

(1) the order is capable of being adequately compensated for by money; or

(2) any prejudice caused by the making of the order is outweighed by the benefit accruing from the order to the persons who have access to the telecommunications system.

The court must consider this application in the light of the principle that no person should unreasonably be denied access to a telecommunications system.

The court has the power under paragraph 5 to modify or impose such conditions as it sees fit in the order. Any rights granted by the order over the land must be exercised in a way that ensures the least possible loss and damage is caused.

It can be seen that this a form of compulsory purchase of rights.

To date, the major telecommunications operators have not used their powers under paragraph 5 widely, possibly because of concern about the adverse effect such use, if widespread, would have on their public image.

12.4   REINSTATEMENT UNDER THE CODE – PARAGRAPHS 20 AND 21

Paragraphs 20 and 21 are the only means of obtaining removal of apparatus and reinstatement under the Code. The procedures are similar, but can only be exercised in separate circumstances.

Paragraph 20 (development or change of use)

Paragraph 20 allows any person with an interest in the land where telecommunications apparatus is kept or installed, or in adjacent land, to require the alteration of the apparatus by notice given in the operator to enable that person to carry out the proposed improvement of the land. (The definition of 'alteration' under the Code is the moving, removal or replacement of the apparatus.)

The person who has an interest in the land where the telecommunications apparatus is installed or in adjacent land may rely on paragraph 20 only when he requires the alteration of the apparatus in order to develop or change the use of the land. The person must serve a notice on the operator requiring the removal of the apparatus. The operator has 28 days in which to serve a counter notice. If the operator does not serve a counter notice, then the operator must remove the apparatus.

However, if the operator serves a counter notice within the 28-day period, the landowner must apply to court to have the apparatus removed.

The court can only sanction the proposed alteration if it is satisfied that the alteration is necessary in order for the proposed development and change of use to be carried out and that it will not interfere substantially with any service provided by the operator's system. Once again, in considering the application the court must have regard to the principle that no person should unreasonably be denied access to a telecommunications system.

It can be seen that this test is not limited to the issues which would arise were the landlord seeking to regain possession under ground (f) of s 30(1) of the Act (see **4.2** for comments on ground (f)). Even if the owner/landlord can prove that relocation or removal of the apparatus is necessary in order to redevelop, he may still lose if it is found impracticable to relocate the apparatus to a location which would allow the operator's service to be maintained.

Paragraph 21

The provisions of paragraph 21 apply where the land is required for any reason other than re-development. The provisions of this paragraph allow any person to request the removal of an operator's apparatus because:

(1) this is required as a result of any enactment; or

(2) the apparatus is kept on the land without a right binding that person (for example where a tenant or licensee as occupier of the land has granted consent to an operator to install some apparatus, a landlord could seek to reinstate the property); or

(3) for any other reason (for example if the agreement between the occupier and the operator has expired).

As with paragraph 20, the applicant must give notice to the operator demanding removal. Once again, the operator has 28 days to serve a counter notice, and if the operator fails to serve a counter notice the apparatus can be removed.

Paragraph 21 states that if the operator serves a counter notice it must contain either:

(1) a claim that the applicant is not entitled to require the removal of the apparatus; or

(2) details of any steps which the operator proposes to take in order to secure a right against that person to keep the apparatus on the land (for example an application under paragraph 5).

If the operator serves a counter notice, the applicant has to apply to the court for an order to enforce the removal or relocation of the apparatus and the court will only make such an order if it is satisfied that:

(1) the operator is not intending to take those steps set out in its counter notice or is being unreasonably dilatory in taking those steps; or

(2) the steps set out in the counter notice will not secure the operator's right to keep the apparatus on the land.

Note that all notices served by an operator under the Code (including counter notices under paragraphs 20 or 21) must be approved by Oftel.

Note also that a court order under paragraphs 20 or 21 for removal of apparatus will authorise removal by the operator. If the occupier wants to remove the apparatus itself, it must obtain a further order to authorise this.

An occupier who is unsuccessful in an application for removal of apparatus under paragraph 21 is likely to be in the same position as an occupier who receives notice under paragraph 5: in both cases the operator has a right to apply to the court as stated above. It is not clear in a 'renewal' context whether and to what extent the court will take into account the provisions of any previous agreement between the parties, nor how the court will exercise its power under paragraph 7 of the Code to fix the consideration payable. In both paragraph 5 cases and 'renewal' cases, the consideration must be such as 'would have been fair and reasonable if the agreement had been given willingly'. This suggests that open-market evidence would be relevant.

There have been very few, if any, cases where rights under the Code have been either granted or 'renewed' by the court (the authors have not encountered any reported cases). It is possible that a county court judge who was familiar with the operation of the 1954 Act would deal with an application under the Code in a similar way, but of course the vast majority of county court judges will never have tried a contested 1954 Act renewal.

12.5   TIPS FOR OPERATORS

The Code has put all the cards into the operators' hands. How they choose to play them, and how tough an approach they decide to take, will be based largely on their concerns about their public image.

An operator installing new apparatus will want to achieve an economic return and, therefore, will be likely to seek a term at least long enough to amortise the capital costs of installation.

It is advised below that it is in the occupier's interest that any agreement made should be expressly excluded from the security of tenure provisions of the Act. It could be argued that this would also be in the operator's interests, because the operator would only have to deal with one set of proceedings (pursuant to paragraph 21) on expiry.

Ideally, an operator would submit its own draft agreement, prior to obtaining planning permission, preferably seeking fully qualified rights in respect of alterations, site sharing etc, with a view to obtaining a commitment from the occupier as early as possible, and leaving much of the detail to be agreed after planning permission had been obtained.

Particular complications arise when the operator is negotiating with an occupier which is a lessee.

(1) Check the extent of the occupier's demise. If apparatus is to be placed on the roof, does the demise include the airspace? If the installation of the apparatus involves drilling holes into the structure, is the structure within the demise? If the building in question is multi-let, it almost certainly will not be within the demise.

(2) Check how any electricity to power the apparatus will be supplied. Are the occupier's rights under its lease broad enough to include providing services to third parties?

(3) If the occupier signs an agreement in breach of its lease, the operator will have the benefit of the Code, but the occupier may be vulnerable to forfeiture. Consider whether any indemnity to be given to the occupier would extend to the costs of seeking relief from forfeiture and for the occupier's loss of profit if it loses and has to relocate.

12.6   TIPS FOR OCCUPIERS

(1) Ideally, the occupier should resist entering into any commitment until the planning permission has been obtained as this is the point at which the site

becomes valuable to other operators; one option is for the occupier to make the application.

(2) The occupier should avoid signing any document allowing the operator to have access pending completion of formal documentation. The Code will apply to that prior document, and it may well be in the operator's interests to refuse to sign anything more restrictive.

(3) If the formal document grants the occupier exclusive possession of an area, for a period of time, in return for a payment, it will almost certainly be treated in law as a lease, even if it is described as a licence or an agreement. Confusion can be minimised by describing the document as a lease. That lease should be excluded from the security of tenure provisions of the Act. This will not prevent the Code from applying, but it will mean that the occupier has only one set of hoops through which to jump on expiry.

(4) The occupier should aim to tie down the operator to a detailed specification of all the apparatus, equipment, wiring etc that will be required and the specification should include details of the enabling works and access arrangements during the construction phase and reinstatement at the end of the construction phase. This should avoid arguments later and also will open up the scope to negotiate additional rent for the installation of further equipment.

(5) The operator will normally seek a term long enough to amortise the capital cost of installation. If a term of more than 5 years is agreed there should be provisions for rent review. Consider whether index-linking or a review based on open-market comparables is likely to produce a higher income; if possible, the occupier should protect its position by reserving the right to review on whichever basis produces the higher result.

(6) Rent reviews normally provide for the effect on rent of tenant's improvements to be disregarded. In telecommunications cases, it is more than arguable that the operator is paying for a right to install specified apparatus, and if it is to be given the right to install additional apparatus, it should be required to pay a higher rent. This can be achieved either by defining the apparatus which can be installed, with the parties negotiating a new rent if the operator wants to install additional apparatus, or by giving the operator a right to install additional apparatus but with that being specifically taken into account on review (obviously, a review based solely on index-linking an initial sum will not achieve this). The first of these options will be better for the occupier, because it will not have to wait until the next review to receive an increased income.

(7) The Code does not stipulate provisions which parties can or cannot include. The occupier may want to include a break clause if it intends to redevelop the site; this would allow the lease to be determined, but the

occupier would still have to prove its case under paragraph 20. Similarly, the lease can include provisions for compensation if the operator refuses to remove the apparatus on expiry (subject to the general law against contractual penalties – any compensation contracted for must be a genuine pre-estimate of the occupier's probable loss, to the extent that this can be calculated).

(8) The occupier should try to obtain a wide-ranging indemnity from the operator and an obligation on the operator to maintain adequate public liability insurance and to comply with all health and safety legislation. There is active scientific debate about the possible long-term effect of microwave radiation on human health.

(9) The occupier should include a covenant by the operator not to use its apparatus in a way which causes interference to equipment being operated by the occupier – this will be particularly relevant if the apparatus is to be installed in or on an office block. If the operator demands a similar clause from the occupier, this should be resisted because it may inhibit the operator's use of and/or letting income from office premises as technology develops. It may be difficult to reach agreement on this point.

(10)Remember that any forfeiture clause will be subject to paragraph 21 of the Code.

(11)If the occupier is a lessee, it will be prudent for it to seek the consent of its lessor before entering into any document or allowing the operator to start installing apparatus. The vast majority of commercial leases will contain qualified covenants requiring the landlord's prior consent (which may not be withheld unreasonably) to alterations, underletting and/or parting with or sharing possession and an absolute covenant not to allow third parties' rights to be acquired. Breaches of these expose the lessee to a risk of forfeiture and to a, possibly more real, risk of a claim for damages.

(12)Finally, even if the arrangement between the operator and the occupier is a lease excluded from the security of tenure provisions of the Act, bear in mind that the court procedures necessary to remove or relocate the apparatus could take just as long as a renewal opposed on ground (f) of s 30(1) of the Landlord and Tenant Act 1954.

Appendix 1

NOTICES

Landlord's Section 40 Notice– Landlord's Request for Information about Occupation and Sub-tenencies   113

Section 25 Notice – Landlord's Notice Ending a Business Tenancy with Proposals for a new one   117

Section 25 Notice – Landlord's Notice Ending a Business Tenancy and Reasons for Refusing a new one   121

Section 26 Request – Tenant's Request for a New Business Tenancy   125

Tenant's Section 40 Notice – Tenant's Request for Information from Landlord or Landlord's Mortgagee About Landlord's Interest   129

Landlord's Section 26 Counter Notice   131

LANDLORD'S SECTION 40 NOTICE

Landlord and Tenant Act 1954, Part 2 (Notices) Regulations 2004, Form 4

LANDLORD AND TENANT ACT 1954
Section 40(1)

Landlord's Request for Information About Occupation and Sub-Tenancies

(1) Insert name and address of tenant.

To(1)

(2) Insert name and address of landlord.

From(2)

(3) Insert address or description of premises.

1. This notice relates to the following premises(3)

2. I give you notice under section 40(1) of the Landlord and Tenant Act 1954 that I require you to provide information-

(a) by answering questions (1) to (3) in the Table below;

(b) if you answer "yes" to question (2), by giving me the name and address of the person or persons concerned;

(c) if you answer "yes" to question (3), by also answering questions (4) to (10) in the Table below;

(d) if you answer "no" to question (8), by giving me the name and address of the sub-tenant; and

(e) if you answer "yes" to question (10), by giving me details of the notice or request.

TABLE

(1) Do you occupy the premises or any part of them wholly or partly for the purposes of a business that is carried on by you?
(2) To the best of your knowledge and belief, does any other person own an interest in reversion in any part of the premises?
(3) Does your tenancy have effect subject to any sub-tenancy on which your tenancy is immediately expectant?
(4) What premises are comprised in the sub-tenancy?
(5) For what term does it have effect or, if it is terminable by notice, by what notice can it be terminated?
(6) What is the rent payable under it?
(7) Who is the sub-tenant?
(8) To the best of your knowledge and belief, is the sub-tenant in occupation of the premises or of part of the premises comprised in the sub-tenancy?
(9) Is an agreement in force excluding, in relation to the sub-tenancy, the provisions of sections 24 to 28 of the Landlord and Tenant Act 1954?
(10) Has a notice been given under section 25 or 26(6) of that Act, or has a request been made under section 26 of that Act, in relation to the sub-tenancy?

L&T28/1

3. You must give the information concerned in writing and within the period of one month beginning with the date of service of this notice.

4. Please send all correspondence about this notice to:

Name:

Address:

Signed: Date:

(4) Delete
whichever is
inapplicable.

(4)[Landlord](4)[On behalf of the landlord]

IMPORTANT NOTE FOR THE TENANT

This notice contains some words and phrases that you may not understand. The Notes below should help you, but it would be wise to seek professional advice, for example, from a solicitor or surveyor, before responding to this notice.

Once you have provided the information required by this notice, you must correct it if you realise that it is not, or is no longer, correct. This obligation lasts for six months from the date of service of this notice, but an exception is explained in the next paragraph. If you need to correct information already given, you must do so within one month of becoming aware that the information is incorrect.

The obligation will cease if, after transferring your tenancy, you notify the landlord of the transfer and of the name and address of the person to whom your tenancy has been transferred.

If you fail to comply with the requirements of this notice, or the obligation mentioned above, you may face civil proceedings for breach of the statutory duty that arises under section 40 of the Landlord and Tenant Act 1954. In any such proceedings a court may order you to comply with that duty and may make an award of damages.

NOTES

The sections mentioned below are sections of the Landlord and Tenant Act 1954, as amended, (most recently by the Regulatory Reform (Business Tenancies) (England and Wales) Order 2003).

Purpose of this notice

Your landlord (or, if he or she is a tenant, possibly your landlord's landlord) has sent you this notice in order to obtain information about your occupation and that of any sub-tenants. This information may be relevant to the taking of steps to end or renew your business tenancy.

Time limit for replying

You must provide the relevant information within one month of the date of service of this notice (section 40(1), (2) and (5)).

L&T28/2

Information required

You do not have to give your answers on this form; you may use a separate sheet for this purpose. The notice requires you to provide, in writing, information in the form of answers to questions (1) to (3) in the Table above and, if you answer "yes" to question (3), also to provide information in the form of answers to questions (4) to (10) in that Table. Depending on your answer to question (2) and, if applicable in your case, questions (8) and (10), you must also provide the information referred to in paragraph 2(b), (d) and (e) of this notice. Question (2) refers to a person who owns an interest in reversion. You should answer "yes" to this question if you know or believe that there is a person who receives, or is entitled to receive, rent in respect of any part of the premises (other than the landlord who served this notice).

When you answer questions about sub-tenants, please bear in mind that, for these purposes, a sub-tenant includes a person retaining possession of premises by virtue of the Rent (Agriculture) Act 1976 or the Rent Act 1977 after the coming to an end of a sub-tenancy, and "sub-tenancy" includes a right so to retain possession (section 40(8)).

You should keep a copy of your answers and of any other information provided in response to questions (2), (8) or (10) above.

If, once you have given this information, you realise that it is not, or is no longer, correct, you must give the correct information within one month of becoming aware that the previous information is incorrect. Subject to the next paragraph, your duty to correct any information that you have already given continues for six months after you receive this notice (section 40(5)). You should give the correct information to the landlord who gave you this notice unless you receive notice of the transfer of his or her interest, and of the name and address of the person to whom that interest has been transferred. In that case, the correct information must be given to that person.

If you transfer your tenancy within the period of six months referred to above, your duty to correct information already given will cease if you notify the landlord of the transfer and of the name and address of the person to whom your tenancy has been transferred.

If you do not provide the information requested, or fail to correct information that you have provided earlier, after realising that it is not, or is no longer, correct, proceedings may be taken against you and you may have to pay damages (section 40B).

If you are in any doubt about the information that you should give, get immediate advice from a solicitor or a surveyor.

Validity of this notice

The landlord who has given you this notice may not be the landlord to whom you pay your rent (sections 44 and 67). This does not necessarily mean that the notice is invalid.

If you have any doubts about whether this notice is valid, get advice immediately from a solicitor or a surveyor.

Further information

An explanation of the main points to consider when renewing or ending a business tenancy, "Renewing and Ending Business Leases: a Guide for Tenants and Landlords", can be found at www.odpm.gov.uk. Printed copies of the explanation, but not of this form, are available from 1st June 2004 from Free Literature. PO Box 236, Wetherby, West Yorkshire, LS23 7NB (0870 1226 236).

SECTION 25 NOTICES

Landlord and Tenant Act 1954 Part 2 (Notices) Regulations 2004, Form 1

LANDLORD AND TENANT ACT 1954

Section 25

Landlord's Notice Ending a Business Tenancy with Proposals for a New One

> **IMPORTANT NOTE FOR THE LANDLORD:**
> If you are willing to grant a new tenancy, complete this form and send it to the tenant. If you wish to oppose the grant of a new tenancy, use form 2 (Oyez Form L&T 25(2)) in Schedule 2 to the Landlord and Tenant Act 1954, Part 2 (Notices) Regulations 2004 or, where the tenant may be entitled to acquire the freehold or an extended lease, form 7 (Oyez Form L&T 24*) in that Schedule, instead of this form.

(1) Insert name and address of tenant.

To (1)

(2) Insert name and address of landlord.

From (2)

(3) Insert address or description of property.

1.   This notice applies to the following property(3)

2.   I am giving you notice under section 25 of the Landlord and Tenant Act 1954 to end your tenancy

(4) Insert date.

on (4)

3.   I am not opposed to granting you a new tenancy. You will find my proposals for the new tenancy, which we can discuss, in the Schedule to this notice.

4.   If we cannot agree on all the terms of a new tenancy, either you or I may ask the court to order the grant of a new tenancy and settle the terms on which we cannot agree.

5.   If you wish to ask the court for a new tenancy you must do so by the date in paragraph 2, unless we agree in writing to a later date and do so before the date in paragraph 2.

6.   Please send all correspondence about this notice to:

Name:

Address:

Signed: Date:

(5) Delete if inapplicable.

(5)[Landlord] (5)[On behalf of the Landlord] (5)[Mortgagee] (5)[On behalf of the mortgagee]

[P.T.O.

L&T25(1)/1

SCHEDULE

LANDLORD'S PROPOSALS FOR A NEW TENANCY (6)

L&T25(1)/2

IMPORTANT NOTE FOR THE TENANT

This Notice is intended to bring your tenancy to an end. If you want to continue to occupy your property after the date specified in paragraph 2 you must act quickly. If you are in any doubt about the action that you should take, get advice immediately from a solicitor or a surveyor.

The landlord is prepared to offer you a new tenancy and has set out proposed terms in the Schedule to this notice. <u>You are not bound to accept these terms.</u> They are merely suggestions as a basis for negotiation. In the event of disagreement, ultimately the court would settle the terms of the new tenancy.

It would be wise to seek professional advice before agreeing to accept the landlord's terms or putting forward your own proposals.

NOTES

The sections mentioned below are sections of the Landlord and Tenant Act 1954, as amended, (most recently by the Regulatory Reform (Business Tenancies) (England and Wales) Order 2003)

Ending of tenancy and grant of new tenancy

This notice is intended to bring your tenancy to an end on the date given in paragraph 2. Section 25 contains rules about the date that the landlord can put in that paragraph.

However, your landlord is prepared to offer you a new tenancy and has set out proposals for it in the Schedule to this notice (section 25(8)). You are not obliged to accept these proposals and may put forward your own.

If you and your landlord are unable to agree terms either one of you may apply to the court. You may not apply to the court if your landlord has already done so (section 24(2A)). If you wish to apply to the court you must do so by the date given in paragraph 2 of this notice, unless you and your landlord have agreed in writing to extend the deadline (sections 29A and 29B).

The court will settle the rent and other terms of the new tenancy or those on which you and your landlord cannot agree (sections 34 and 35). If you apply to the court your tenancy will continue after the date shown in paragraph 2 of this notice while your application is being considered (section 24).

If you are in any doubt about what action you should take, get advice immediately from a solicitor or a surveyor.

Negotiating a new tenancy

Most tenancies are renewed by negotiation. You and your landlord may agree in writing to extend the deadline for making an application to the court while negotiations continue. Either you or your landlord can ask the court to fix the rent that you will have to pay while the tenancy continues (sections 24A to 24D).

You may only stay in the property after the date in paragraph 2 (or if we have agreed in writing to a later date, that date), if by then you or the landlord has asked the court to order the grant of a new tenancy.

If you do try to agree a new tenancy with your landlord remember:

- that your present tenancy will not continue after the date in paragraph 2 of this notice without the agreement in writing mentioned above, unless you have applied to the court or your landlord has done so, and

- that you will lose your right to apply to the court once the deadline in paragraph 2 of this notice has passed, unless there is a written agreement extending the deadline.

Validity of this notice

The landlord who has given you this notice may not be the landlord to whom you pay your rent (sections 44 and 67). This does not necessarily mean that the notice is invalid.

If you have any doubts about whether this notice is valid, get advice immediately from a solicitor or a surveyor.

Further information

An explanation of the main points to consider when renewing or ending a business tenancy, "Renewing and Ending Business Leases: a Guide for Tenants and Landlords", can be found at www.odpm.gov.uk. Printed copies of the explanation, but not of this form, are available from 1st June 2004 from Free Literature, PO Box 236, Wetherby, West Yorkshire, LS23 7NB (0870 1226 236).

L&T25(1)/3

Landlord and Tenant Act 1954, Part 2 (Notices) Regulations 2004, Form 2

LANDLORD AND TENANT ACT 1954
Section 25
Landlord's Notice Ending a Business Tenancy and Reasons for Refusing a New One

---

IMPORTANT NOTE FOR THE LANDLORD:

If you wish to oppose the grant of a new tenancy on any of the grounds in section 30(1) of the Landlord and Tenant Act 1954, complete this form and send it to the tenant. If the tenant may be entitled to acquire the freehold or an extended lease, use form 7 (Oyez Form L&T 24*) in Schedule 2 to the Landlord and Tenant Act 1954, Part 2 (Notices) Regulations 2004 instead of this form.

---

(1) Insert name and address of tenant.

To (1)

(2) Insert name and address of landlord.

From (2)

(3) Insert address or description of the property.

1.   This notice relates to the following property(3)

2.   I am giving you notice under section 25 of the Landlord and Tenant Act 1954 to end your tenancy

(4) Insert date.

on (4)

3.   I am opposed to the grant of a new tenancy.

4.   You may ask the court to order the grant of a new tenancy. If you do, I will oppose your application

(5) Insert letter(s) of the paragraph(s) relied on.

on the ground(s) mentioned in paragraph(s)(5)   of section 30(1) of that Act. I draw your attention to the Table in the Notes below, which sets out all the grounds of opposition.

5. If you wish to ask the court for a new tenancy you must do so before the date in paragraph 2 unless, before that date, we agree in writing to a later date.

6. I can ask the court to order the ending of your tenancy without granting you a new tenancy. I may have to pay you compensation if I have relied only on one or more of the grounds mentioned in paragraphs (e), (f) and (g) of section 30(1). If I ask the court to end your tenancy, you can challenge my application.

7. Please send all correspondence about this notice to:

Name:

Address:

Signed: Date:

(6) Delete if inapplicable.

(6)[Landlord] (6)[On behalf of the landlord] (6)[Mortgagee] (6)[On behalf of the mortgagee]

[P.T.O.

L&T25(2)/1

IMPORTANT NOTE FOR THE TENANT

This notice is intended to bring your tenancy to an end on the date specified in paragraph 2.

Your landlord is not prepared to offer you a new tenancy. <u>You will not get a new tenancy unless you successfully challenge in court the grounds on which your landlord opposes the grant of a new tenancy</u>.

If you want to continue to occupy your property you must act quickly. The notes below should help you to decide what action you now need to take. If you want to challenge your landlord's refusal to renew your tenancy, get advice immediately from a solicitor or a surveyor.

NOTES

The sections mentioned below are sections of the Landlord and Tenant Act 1954, as amended, (most recently by the Regulatory Reform (Business Tenancies) (England and Wales) Order 2003)

Ending of your tenancy

This notice is intended to bring your tenancy to an end on the date given in paragraph 2. Section 25 contains rules about the date that the landlord can put in that paragraph.

Your landlord is not prepared to offer you a new tenancy. If you want a new tenancy you will need to apply to the court for a new tenancy and successfully challenge the landlord's grounds for opposition (see the section below headed *"Landlord's opposition to new tenancy"*). If you wish to apply to the court you must do so before the date given in paragraph 2 of this notice, unless you and your landlord have agreed in writing, before that date, to extend the deadline (sections 29A and 29B).

If you apply to the court your tenancy will continue after the date given in paragraph 2 of this notice while your application is being considered (section 24). You may not apply to the court if your landlord has already done so (section 24(2A) and (2B)).

You may only stay in the property after the date given in paragraph 2 (or such later date as you and the landlord may have agreed in writing) if before that date you have asked the court to order the grant of a new tenancy or the landlord has asked the court to order the ending of your tenancy without granting you a new one.

If you are in any doubt what action you should take, get advice immediately from a solicitor or a surveyor.

Landlord's opposition to new tenancy

If you apply to the court for a new tenancy, the landlord can only oppose your application on one or more of the grounds set out in section 30(1). If you match the letter(s) specified in paragraph 4 of this notice with those in the first column in the Table below, you can see from the second column the ground(s) on which the landlord relies.

Paragraph of section 30(1)	Grounds
(a)	Where under the current tenancy the tenant has any obligations as respects the repair and maintenance of the holding, that the tenant ought not to be granted a new tenancy in view of the state of repair of the holding, being a state resulting from the tenant's failure to comply with the said obligations.
(b)	That the tenant ought not to be granted a new tenancy in view of his persistent delay in paying rent which has become due.
(c)	That the tenant ought not to be granted a new tenancy in view of other substantial breaches by him or her of his obligations under the current tenancy, or for any other reason connected with the tenant's use or management of the holding.
(d)	That the landlord has offered and is willing to provide or secure the provision of alternative accommodation for the tenant, that the terms on which the alternative accommodation is available are reasonable having regard to the terms of the current tenancy and to all other relevant circumstances, and that the accommodation and the time at which it will be available are suitable for the tenant's requirements (including the requirement to preserve goodwill) having regard to the nature and class of his or her business and to the situation and extent of, and facilities afforded by, the holding.

L&T25(2)/2

(e)	Where the current tenancy was created by the sub-letting of part only of the property comprised in a superior tenancy and the landlord is the owner of an interest in reversion expectant on the termination of that superior tenancy, that the aggregate of the rents reasonably obtainable on separate lettings of the holding and the remainder of that property would be substantially less than the rent reasonably obtainable on a letting of that property as a whole, that on the termination of the current tenancy the landlord requires possession of the holding for the purposes of letting or otherwise disposing of the said property as a whole, and that in view thereof the tenant ought not to be granted a new tenancy.
(f)	That on the termination of the current tenancy the landlord intends to demolish or reconstruct the premises comprised in the holding or a substantial part of those premises or to carry out substantial work of construction on the holding or part thereof and that he or she could not reasonably do so without obtaining possession of the holding.
(g)	On the termination of the current tenancy the landlord intends to occupy the holding for the purposes, or partly for the purposes, of a business to be carried on by him or her therein, or as his or her residence.

In this Table "the holding" means the property that is the subject of the tenancy.

In ground (e), "the landlord is the owner of an interest in reversion expectant on the termination of that superior tenancy" means that the landlord has an interest in the property that will entitle him or her, when your immediate landlord's tenancy comes to an end, to exercise certain rights and obligations in relation to the property that are currently exercisable by your immediate landlord.

If the landlord relies on ground (f), the court can sometimes still grant a new tenancy if certain conditions set out in section 31A are met.

If the landlord relies on ground (g), please note that "the landlord" may have an extended meaning. Where a landlord has a controlling interest in a company then either the landlord or the company can rely on ground (g). Where the landlord is a company and a person has a controlling interest in that company then either of them can rely on ground (g) (section 30(1A) and (1B)). A person has a "controlling interest" in a company if, had he been a company, the other company would have been its subsidiary (section 46(2)).

The landlord must normally have been the landlord for at least five years before he or she can rely on ground (g).

Compensation

If you cannot get a new tenancy solely because one or more of grounds (e), (f) and (g) applies, you may be entitled to compensation under section 37. If your landlord has opposed your application on any of the other grounds as well as (e), (f) or (g) you can only get compensation if the court's refusal to grant a new tenancy is based solely on one or more of grounds (e), (f) and (g). In other words, you cannot get compensation under section 37 if the court has refused your tenancy on *other* grounds, even if one or more of grounds (e), (f) and (g) also applies.

If your landlord is an authority possessing compulsory purchase powers (such as a local authority) you may be entitled to a disturbance payment under Part 3 of the Land Compensation Act 1973.

Validity of this notice

The landlord who has given you this notice may not be the landlord to whom you pay your rent (sections 44 and 67). This does not necessarily mean that the notice is invalid.

If you have any doubts about whether this notice is valid, get advice immediately from a solicitor or a surveyor.

Further information

An explanation of the main points to consider when renewing or ending a business tenancy, "Renewing and Ending Business Leases: a Guide for Tenants and Landlords", can be found at www.odpm.gov.uk. Printed copies of the explanation, but not of this form, are available from 1st June 2004 from Free Literature, PO Box 236, Wetherby, West Yorkshire, LS23 7NB (0870 1226 236).

L&T25(2)/3

SECTION 26 REQUEST

Landlord and Tenant Act 1954, Part 2 (Notices) Regulations 2004, Form 3

LANDLORD AND TENANT ACT 1954

Section 26

Tenant's Request for a New Business Tenancy

(1) Insert name and address of landlord.

To (1)

(2) Insert name and address of tenant.

From (2)

(3) Insert address or description of the property.

1.   This notice relates to the following property (3)

(4) Insert date.

2.   I am giving you notice under section 26 of the Landlord and Tenant Act 1954 that I request a new tenancy beginning on (4)

3.   You will find my proposals for the new tenancy, which we can discuss, in the Schedule to this notice.

4.   If we cannot agree on all the terms of a new tenancy, either you or I may ask the court to order the grant of a new tenancy and settle the terms on which we cannot agree.

5.   If you wish to ask the court to order the grant of a new tenancy you must do so by the date in paragraph 2, unless we agree in writing to a later date and do so before the date in paragraph 2.

6.   You may oppose my request for a new tenancy only on one or more of the grounds set out in section 30(1) of the Landlord and Tenant Act 1954. You must tell me what your grounds are within two months of receiving this notice. If you miss this deadline you will not be able to oppose renewal of my tenancy and you will have to grant me a new tenancy.

7.   Please send all correspondence about this notice to:

Name:

Address:

Signed: Date:

(5) Delete whichever is inapplicable.

(5)[Tenant] (5)[On behalf of the tenant]

[P.T.O.

L&T26/1

SCHEDULE

TENANT'S PROPOSALS FOR A NEW TENANCY(6)

(6) Attach
or insert
proposed
terms of the
new tenancy.

IMPORTANT NOTE FOR THE LANDLORD

This notice requests a new tenancy of your property or part of it. If you want to oppose this request you must act quickly.

Read the notice and all the Notes carefully. It would be wise to seek professional advice.

[P.T.O.

L&T26/2

NOTES

The sections mentioned below are sections of the Landlord and Tenant Act 1954, as amended, (most recently by the Regulatory Reform (Business Tenancies) (England and Wales) Order 2003)

Tenant's request for a new tenancy

This request by your tenant for a new tenancy brings his or her current tenancy to an end on the day before the date mentioned in paragraph 2 of this notice. Section 26 contains rules about the date that the tenant can put in paragraph 2 of this notice.

Your tenant can apply to the court under section 24 for a new tenancy. You may apply for a new tenancy yourself, under the same section, but not if your tenant has already served an application. Once an application has been made to the court, your tenant's current tenancy will continue after the date mentioned in paragraph 2 while the application is being considered by the court. Either you or your tenant can ask the court to fix the rent which your tenant will have to pay whilst the tenancy continues (sections 24A to 24D). The court will settle any terms of a new tenancy on which you and your tenant disagree (sections 34 and 35).

Time limit for opposing your tenant's request

If you do not want to grant a new tenancy, you have <u>two months from the making of your tenant's request</u> in which to notify him or her that you will oppose any application made to the court for a new tenancy. You do not need a special form to do this, but <u>the notice must be in writing and it must state on which of the grounds set out in section 30(1) you will oppose the application</u>. If you do not use the same wording of the ground (or grounds), as set out below, your notice may be ineffective.

If there has been any delay in your seeing this notice, you may need to act very quickly. If you are in any doubt about what action you should take, get advice immediately from a solicitor or a surveyor.

Grounds for opposing tenant's application

If you wish to oppose the renewal of the tenancy, you can do so by opposing your tenant's application to the court, or by making your own application to the court for termination without renewal. However, you can only oppose your tenant's application, or apply for termination without renewal, on one or more of the grounds set out in section 30(1). These grounds are set out below. <u>You will only be able to rely on the ground(s) of opposition that you have mentioned in your written notice to your tenant.</u>

In this Table "the holding" means the property that is the subject of the tenancy.

Paragraph of section 30(1)	Grounds
(a)	Where under the current tenancy the tenant has any obligations as respects the repair and maintenance of the holding, that the tenant ought not to be granted a new tenancy in view of the state of repair of the holding, being a state resulting from the tenant's failure to comply with the said obligations.
(b)	That the tenant ought not to be granted a new tenancy in view of his or her persistent delay in paying rent which has become due.
(c)	That the tenant ought not to be granted a new tenancy in view of other substantial breaches by him or her of his or her obligations under the current tenancy, or for any other reason connected with the tenant's use or management of the holding.
(d)	That the landlord has offered and is willing to provide or secure the provision of alternative accommodation for the tenant, that the terms on which the alternative accommodation is available are reasonable having regard to the terms of the current tenancy and to all other relevant circumstances, and that the accommodation and the time at which it will be available are suitable for the tenant's requirements (including the requirement to preserve goodwill) having regard to the nature and class of his business and to the situation and extent of, and facilities afforded by, the holding.

(e)	Where the current tenancy was created by the sub-letting of part only of the property comprised in a superior tenancy and the landlord is the owner of an interest in reversion expectant on the termination of that superior tenancy, that the aggregate of the rents reasonably obtainable on separate lettings of the holding and the remainder of that property would be substantially less than the rent reasonably obtainable on a letting of that property as a whole, that on the termination of the current tenancy the landlord requires possession of the holding for the purposes of letting or otherwise disposing of the said property as a whole, and that in view thereof the tenant ought not to be granted a new tenancy.
(f)	That on the termination of the current tenancy the landlord intends to demolish or reconstruct the premises comprised in the holding or a substantial part of those premises or to carry out substantial work of construction on the holding or part thereof and that he or she could not reasonably do so without obtaining possession of the holding.
(g)	On the termination of the current tenancy the landlord intends to occupy the holding for the purposes, or partly for the purposes, of a business to be carried on by him or her therein, or as his or her residence.

Compensation

If your tenant cannot get a new tenancy solely because one or more of grounds (e), (f) and (g) applies, he or she is entitled to compensation under section 37. If you have opposed your tenant's application on any of the other grounds mentioned in section 30(1), as well as on one or more of grounds (e), (f) and (g), your tenant can only get compensation if the court's refusal to grant a new tenancy is based solely on ground (e), (f) or (g). In other words, your tenant cannot get compensation under section 37 if the court has refused the tenancy on *other* grounds, even if one or more of grounds (e), (f) and (g) also applies.

If you are an authority possessing compulsory purchase powers (such as a local authority), your tenant may be entitled to a disturbance payment under Part 3 of the Land Compensation Act 1973.

Negotiating a new tenancy

Most tenancies are renewed by negotiation and your tenant has set out proposals for the new tenancy in paragraph 3 of this notice. You are not obliged to accept these proposals and may put forward your own. You and your tenant may agree in writing to extend the deadline for making an application to the court while negotiations continue. Your tenant may not apply to the court for a new tenancy until two months have passed from the date of the making of the request contained in this notice, unless you have already given notice opposing your tenant's request as mentioned in paragraph 6 of this notice (section 29A(3)).

If you try to agree a new tenancy with your tenant, remember:

- that one of you will need to apply to the court before the date in paragraph 2 of this notice, unless you both agree to extend the period for making an application.

- that any such agreement must be in writing and must be made before the date in paragraph 2 (sections 29A and 29B).

Validity of this notice

The tenant who has given you this notice may not be the person from whom you receive rent (sections 44 and 67). This does not necessarily mean that the notice is invalid.

If you have any doubts about whether this notice is valid, get advice immediately from a solicitor or a surveyor.

Further information

An explanation of the main points to consider when renewing or ending a business tenancy, "Renewing and Ending Business Leases: a Guide for Tenants and Landlords", can be found at www.odpm.gov.uk. Printed copies of the explanation, but not of this form, are available from 1st June 2004 from Free Literature, PO Box 236, Wetherby, West Yorkshire, LS23 7NB (0870 1226 236).

Oyez 7 Spa Road, London SE16 3QQ   **Landlord and Tenant 26**   6.2004   5059805   L&T26/4

TENANT'S SECTION 40 NOTICE

Landlord and Tenant Act 1954, Part 2 (Notices) Regulations 2004, Form 5

LANDLORD AND TENANT ACT 1954
Section 40(3)

Tenant's Request for Information from Landlord or Landlord's Mortgagee About Landlord's Interest

(1) Insert name and address of reversioner or reversioner's mortgagee in possession. (See the first note below.)

(2) Insert name and address of tenant.

To(1)

From(2)

1. This notice relates to the follow premises(3)

(3) Insert address or description of premises.

2. In accordance with section 40(3) of the Landlord and Tenant Act 1954 I require you-

(a) to state in writing whether you are the owner of the fee simple in respect of the premises or any part of them or the mortgagee in possession of such an owner,

(b) if you answer "no" to (a), to state in writing, to the best of your knowledge and belief-

(i) the name and address of the person who is your or, as the case may be, your mortgagor's immediate landlord in respect of the premises or of the part in respect of which you are not, or your mortgagor is not, the owner in fee simple;

(ii) for what term your or your mortgagor's tenancy has effect and what is the earliest date (if any) at which that tenancy is terminable by notice to quit given by the landlord; and

(iii) whether a notice has been given under section 25 or 26(6) of the Landlord and Tenant Act 1954, or a request has been made under section 26 of that Act, in relation to the tenancy and, if so, details of the notice or request;

(c) to state in writing, to the best of your knowledge and belief, the name and address of any other person who owns an interest in reversion in any part of the premises;

(d) if you are a reversioner, to state in writing whether there is a mortgagee in possession of your interest in the premises; and

(e) if you answer "yes" to (d), to state in writing, to the best of your knowledge and belief, the name and address of the mortgagee in possession.

3. You must give the information concerned within the period of one month beginning with the date of service of this notice.

4. Please send all correspondence about this notice to:

Name:

Address:

Signed: Date:

(4) Delete whichever is inapplicable.

(4)[Tenant](4)[On behalf of the tenant]

L&T29*/1

IMPORTANT NOTE FOR LANDLORD OR LANDLORD'S MORTGAGEE

This notice contains some words and phrases that you may not understand. The Notes below should help you, but it would be wise to seek professional advice, for example, from a solicitor or surveyor, before responding to this notice.

Once you have provided the information required by this notice, you must correct it if you realise that it is not, or is no longer, correct. This obligation lasts for six months from the date of service of this notice, but an exception is explained in the next paragraph. If you need to correct information already given, you must do so within one month of becoming aware that the information is incorrect.

The obligation will cease if, after transferring your interest, you notify the tenant of the transfer and of the name and address of the person to whom your interest has been transferred.

If you fail to comply with the requirements of this notice, or the obligation mentioned above, you may face civil proceedings for breach of the statutory duty that arises under section 40 of the Landlord and Tenant Act 1954. In any such proceedings a court may order you to comply with that duty and may make an award of damages.

NOTES

The sections mentioned below are sections of the Landlord and Tenant Act 1954, as amended, (most recently by the Regulatory Reform (Business Tenancies) (England and Wales) Order 2003)

Terms used in this notice

The following terms, which are used in paragraph 2 of this notice, are defined in section 40(8):

> "mortgagee in possession" includes a receiver appointed by the mortgagee or by the court who is in receipt of the rents and profits;

> "reversioner" means any person having an interest in the premises, being an interest in reversion expectant (whether immediately or not) on the tenancy; and

> "reversioner's mortgagee in possession" means any person being a mortgagee in possession in respect of such an interest.

Section 40(8) requires the reference in paragraph 2(b) of this notice to your mortgagor to be read in the light of the definition of "mortgagee in possession".

A mortgagee (mortgage lender) will be "in possession" if the mortgagor (the person who owes money to the mortgage lender) has failed to comply with the terms of the mortgage. The mortgagee may then be entitled to receive rent that would normally have been paid to the mortgagor.

The term "the owner of the fee simple" means the freehold owner.

The term "reversioner" includes the freehold owner and any intermediate landlord as well as the immediate landlord of the tenant who served this notice.

Purpose of this notice and information required

This notice requires you to provide, in writing, the information requested in paragraph 2(a) and (c) of the notice and, if applicable in your case, in paragraph 2(b), (d) and (e). You do not need to use a special form for this purpose.

If, once you have given this information, you realise that it is not, or is no longer, correct, you must give the correct information within one month of becoming aware that the previous information is incorrect. Subject to the last paragraph in this section of these Notes, your duty to correct any information that you have already given continues for six months after you receive this notice (section 40(5)).

You should give the correct information to the tenant who gave you this notice unless you receive notice of the transfer of his or her interest, and of the name and address of the person to whom that interest has been transferred. In that case, the correct information must be given to that person.

If you do not provide the information requested, or fail to correct information that you have provided earlier, after realising that it is not, or is no longer, correct, proceedings may be taken against you and you may have to pay damages (section 40B).

If you are in any doubt as to the information that you should give, get advice immediately from a solicitor or a surveyor.

If you transfer your interest within the period of six months referred to above, your duty to correct information already given will cease if you notify the tenant of that transfer and of the name and address of the person to whom your interest has been transferred.

Time limit for replying

You must provide the relevant information within one month of the date of service of this notice (section 40(3), (4) and (5)).

Validity of this notice

The tenant who has given you this notice may not be the person from whom you receive rent (sections 44 and 67). This does not necessarily mean that the notice is invalid.

If you have any doubts about the validity of the notice, get advice immediately from a solicitor or a surveyor.

Further information

An explanation of the main points to consider when renewing or ending a business tenancy, "Renewing and Ending Business Leases: a Guide for Tenants and Landlords", can be found at www.odpm.gov.uk. Printed copies of the explanation, but not of this form, are available from 1st June 2004 from Free Literature, PO Box 236, Wetherby, West Yorkshire, LS23 7NB (0870 1226 236).

Oyez 7 Spa Road, London SE16 3QQ   **Landlord and Tenant 29***   6.2004

5059815

L&T29*/2

SECTION 26 COUNTER NOTICE

Notice by Landlord

LT8A

in response to Request for a New Tenancy
under Section 26 of the Landlord and Tenant Act 1954

Property	
Landlord	

To	
of	

1.   This notice is given by the Landlord.

2.   It is given in response to the Request dated   which you gave
     under section 26 of the Landlord and Tenant Act 1954 requesting the grant of a new
     tenancy of the Property to commence on   .

3.   If you apply to the Court under Part II of that Act for the grant of a new tenancy,
     [I] [we] will [not oppose your application.] [oppose your application on the grounds
     mentioned in paragraph(s)   of section 30(1) of that Act.]

Signed	

[for and on behalf of the] Landlord

Date	

Name and address of [Landlord] [Landlord's Agent]:

LT8A

Appendix 2

TIMETABLES UNDER THE NEW LAW

The timetables in this Appendix were inspired by papers accompanying a lecture given by Kirk Reynolds as part of a conference organised by Hugo Baring Conferences Ltd some years ago. Those papers set out timetables under the old law.

Landlord wishing to terminate tenancy under Landlord and Tenant Act 1954, Part II   135

Tenant wishing to renew (no sub-tenants)   137

Tenant who has sub-let part and occupies another part wishing to renew   139

LANDLORD WISHING TO TERMINATE TENANCY UNDER LANDLORD AND TENANT ACT 1954, PART II

Stage	Action	Statutory time-limits	Best time
(1)	Compile list of tenants by inspection of the premises, perusal of leases, licences, etc		18–24 months before term expiry date of the lease
(2)	Serve Section 40(1) Notices on all known tenants and sub-tenants	Not more than 2 years before term expiry date of the lease	15–18 months before term date of the lease or sub-lease
(3)	Check replies to Section 40(1) Notices, serve further notices on newly disclosed tenant and sub-tenants	Expiry date	13–15 months before term
(4)	Check current names and addresses of all tenants and sub-tenants (company searches etc)		12–13 months before term expiry date
(5)	Formulate proposals for new term, rent, and other terms of tenancy		In sufficient time for giving the Section 25 Notice
(6)	Serve Section 25 Notices to occupying tenants and sub-tenants, and precautionary notices on absentee tenants and sub-tenants	Not more than 12 months nor more than 6 months before the specified termination date which must not be before the term expiry date (but only if no prior Section 26 Notice from the tenant)	Just under 12 months before the term expiry date (unless there are special reasons to delay)

Stage	*Action*	*Statutory time-limits*	*Best time*
(7)	Check whether tenant's Claim Form has been issued and served	Tenant must issue before the termination date specified in the Section 25 Notice (or such later date as may be agreed) and must serve it within 2 months of the date of issue	
(8)	File an Acknowledgement of Service	Within 14 days of service of tenant's Claim Form	
(9)	Make interim rent application	Must be issued no later than six months after the termination of the relevant tenancy	If interim rent will be higher than the passing rent, apply as early as possible

TENANT WISHING TO RENEW (NO SUB-TENANTS)

Stage	*Action*	*Statutory time-limits*	*Best time*
(1)	Serve notice under s 40(2) on immediate landlord and all known superior landlords	Not more than 2 years before term expiry date	15–18 months before term expiry date
(2)	Check replies to Section 40(2) Notices on newly disclosed superior landlords		13–15 months before term expiry date
(3)	Check names and addresses of all potential competent landlords by company searches etc		12–13 months before term expiry date
(4)	Check whether the competent landlord is still such		Repeat regularly
(5)	Serve a Section 26 Request for new tenancy on your competent landlord	Not more than 12 months before term expiry date of your lease NB: the termination date to be specified should be considered – it can be up to 12 months ahead	Just before the landlord serves a Section 25 Notice on you
(6)	If appropriate, claim compensation for improvements under the Landlord and Tenant Act 1927	Within 3 months of the giving of the Section 25 Notice or (where a Section 26 Request was given) within 3 months of the giving of the landlord's counter notice (or if none was given then 3 months from the time-limit for that counter notice)	At the earliest possible time

Stage	Action	Statutory time-limits	Best time
(7)	Issue and serve Claim Form. Where the competent landlord holds a lease with an unexpired term less than the term you seek (max 15 years), join all appropriate superior landlords in the proceedings	Application must be issued before the termination date specified in the Section 25 Notice or the commencement date for the new tenancy requested in the Section 26 Request (as applicable) (or such later date as may be agreed) and must be served within 2 months of issue	At the earliest possible date

TENANT WHO HAS SUB-LET PART AND OCCUPIES ANOTHER PART WISHING TO RENEW

Stage	Action	Statutory time-limits	Best time
(1)	Compile list of sub-tenants by inspection of the premises, perusal of leases, licences, etc		18–24 months before term expiry date of the sub-lease
(2)	Serve Section 40(1) Notices on all known sub-tenants and sub-sub-tenants	Not more than 2 years before term expiry date of the sub-lease	15–18 months before term expiry date of the sub-lease
(3)	Check replies to Section 40(1) Notices, serve further notices on newly disclosed sub-tenants		13–15 months before term expiry date
(4)	Check current names and addresses of all the tenants and sub-tenants (company searches etc)		12–13 months before term expiry date
(5)	Serve Section 25 Notices on all occupying sub-tenants and sub-sub-tenants, and precautionary notices on absentee sub-tenants and sub-sub-tenants	Not more than 12 months nor more than 6 months before specified termination date which must not be before expiry of term. NB: it must be served before you have a Section 25 Notice from superior lessor or have yourself served a Section 25 Notice on superior lessor or have received a Section 26 Notice from sub-tenant.	Just under 12 months before the term expiry date of the sub-lease, being just over 12 months before the expiry date of your own lease

Thereafter proceed in respect of sub-tenants as per Landlord's Procedure.

Appendix 3

CHECKLISTS OF INFORMATION

Acting for landlord serving Section 25 Notice 143

Acting for landlord who has received Section 26 Request 145

Acting for tenant intending to serve Section 26 Request 147

Acting for tenant who has received Section 25 Notice 151

ACTING FOR LANDLORD SERVING SECTION 25 NOTICE

Client:

A.   INFORMATION REQUIRED

1.   Address and registered office (if different) of client:

Contact name:

Contact telephone number:

2.   Location of original deeds:

    If held by a mortgagee, is consent required for serving/completion?

3.   Name of tenant:

4.1   Is there a superior landlord?

4.2   If so, who is the competent landlord?

5.   Serve Section 40 Notice?

5.1   Before? – Danger of alerting tenant

5.2   At same time?

6.   Are there sub-tenants?

    [Sub-tenants of whole – tenant has no renewal rights – repeat procedure *re* sub-tenants]

    [Sub-tenant(s) of part – is client competent landlord to serve Section 25 Notice on them?]

7.   Address for response to Notice:

8.   Contractual expiry date:

9.   Termination date to be included in the notice?

    –   Not before contractual expiry date

        –   Not less than six months after notice served

        –   Not more than 12 months after notice served

10.1 Does client object to new tenancy?

10.2 If so, on grounds:

11.1 If client does not object to new tenancy, what are its proposals for the new Lease?

11.2 New rent:

11.3 Length of new term:

11.4 Other terms of the new tenancy:

12.1 Passing rent

12.2 Client's view of current market rent – should client push ahead or hold back?

12.3 Is there a last day rent review?

13. Does client want to push ahead by making the court application itself?

B. DIARY DATES

1. Informative:

    1.1   Date of notice

    1.2   Date notice received by tenant (with evidence)

2. DEATH DATE for tenant to issue proceedings for new tenancy (termination date specified in notice)

3. If period for tenant to issue proceedings for new tenancy has been extended, diarise the new DEATH DATE

ACTING FOR LANDLORD WHO HAS RECEIVED SECTION 26 REQUEST

Client:

A.   INFORMATION REQUIRED

1.   Address and registered office (if different) of client:

Contact name:

Contact telephone number:

2.   Location of original deeds:

If held by a mortgagee, is consent required for responding/ proceedings/completion?

3.1   Was request served by correct tenant?

3.2   Serve Section 40 Notice?

4.   Is name of landlord correct?

5.1   Is there a superior landlord?

5.2   If so, who is the competent landlord?

6.   Are there sub-tenants?

[Sub-tenants of whole – tenant has no renewal rights]

[Sub-tenant(s) of part – is client now competent landlord to serve Section 25 Notice on them?]

7.   Contractual expiry date:

8.   Was a valid commencement termination date included in the request?

–   Not before contractual expiry date

–   Not less than six months after notice served

–   Not more than twelve months after notice served

9.   Does client object to new tenancy? If so, on grounds:

10.1 Passing rent:

10.2 Client's view of current market rent – should client push ahead or hold back?

10.3 Is there a last day rent review?

11. Does client want to push ahead by making the court application itself?

B.   DIARY DATES

1. Informative:

1.1 Date of request

1.2 Date request received by client

2. Countdown to counter notice:

    2.1 One month after date of request (one month left to serve)

    2.2 One month and two weeks after date of request (two weeks left to serve)

    2.3 DEATH DATE for service of counter notice if client objects (two months from date of request)

3. Date after which tenant can issue proceedings for a new tenancy (two months after service of request)

4. DEATH DATE for tenant's proceedings for new tenancy (day before commencement date for new tenancy specified in request)

5. If period for tenant to issue proceedings for new tenancy has been extended, diarise the new DEATH DATE

ACTING FOR TENANT INTENDING TO SERVE SECTION 26 REQUEST

Client:

A. INFORMATION REQUIRED

1. Address and registered office (if different) of client:

   Contact name:

   Contact telephone number:

2. Location of original deeds:

   If held by a mortgagee, is consent required for notice/proceedings/completion?

3. Name of the landlord:

4.1 Address and registered office (if different) of landlord:

   Is this the address for payment of rent?

4.2 Is there a superior landlord?

4.3 If so, who is the competent landlord?

4.4 Serve Section 40 Notice?
   (NB: danger of alerting landlord)

5. Are there sub-tenants?

   Sub-tenants of whole – client has no renewal rights [STOP HERE]

   Sub-tenant of part – is client competent landlord to serve Section 25 Notice on them? Should this be done before the Section 26 Request is served?

6. Contractual expiry date:

7. Intended commencement date for new tenancy:

   – Not before contractual expiry date

      – Not less than six months after notice served

      – Not more than 12 months after notice served

7.1 Passing rent:

7.2 Client's view of current market rent – should client push ahead or hold back?

7.3 Is there a last day rent review?

7.4 Would it benefit client to apply for interim rent itself?

8. Have alterations been carried out?

If so – can client claim compensation under the 1927 Act?

– Are alterations to be disregarded when a new rent is fixed under s 34?

B. DIARY DATES

1. Informative:

    1.1 Date of request

    1.2 Date request received by landlord (with evidence)

2. Countdown to landlord's counter notice:

    2.1 One month after date of receipt of request (one month left to serve)

    2.2 One month and two weeks after date of receipt of request (two weeks left to serve)

    2.3 DEATH DATE for service of counter notice (two months from date of receipt of request)

3. Date after which client can issue proceedings for a new tenancy (two months after service of request)

4. Countdown to 1927 Act claim:

    4.1 Two months after date of request (one month left to claim)

    4.2 Two months and two weeks after date of request (two weeks left to claim)

    4.3 DEATH DATE for 1927 Act claim (three months after date of request)

5. Countdown to deadline for proceedings:

    5.1 One month before commencement date for new tenancy as specified in request

5.2   Two weeks before commencement date for new tenancy specified in request

5.3   DEATH DATE for proceedings for new tenancy: day before commencement date for new tenancy specified in request

5.4   If an extension of time for proceedings to be issued is agreed, diarise corresponding dates running up to that deadline

ACTING FOR TENANT WHO HAS RECEIVED SECTION 25 NOTICE

Client:

A. INFORMATION REQUIRED

1. Address and registered office (if different) of client:

   Contact name:

   Contact telephone number:

2. Location of original deeds:

   If held by a mortgagee, is consent required for responding/ proceedings/completion?

3. Was notice addressed to correct tenant?

4.1 Is name of landlord correct?

   Is the address given the address for payment of rent?

4.2 Is there a superior landlord?

4.3 If so, who is the competent landlord?

4.4 Serve Section 40 Notice?

5. Are there sub-tenants?

   Sub-tenants of whole – client has no renewal rights [STOP HERE]

   Sub-tenant of part – is client competent landlord to serve Section 25 Notice on them?

6. Contractual expiry date:

7. Was a valid termination date included in the notice?

   – Not before contractual expiry date

      – Not less than six months after notice served

      – Not more than twelve months after notice served

7.1 Passing rent:

7.2 Client's view of current market rent – should client push ahead or hold back?

7.3　Is there a last day rent review?

7.4　Would it benefit client to apply for interim rent itself?

8.　Have alterations been carried out?

　　If so – can client claim compensation under the 1927 Act?

　　－　Are alterations to be disregarded when a new rent is fixed under s 34?

B.　DIARY DATES

1.　Informative:

　　1.1　Date of notice

　　1.2　Date notice received by client

2.　Countdown to 1927 Act claim:

　　2.1　Two months after date of notice (one month left to claim)

　　2.2　Two months and two weeks after date of notice (two weeks left to claim)

　　2.3　DEATH DATE for 1927 Act claim (three months after date of notice)

3.　Countdown to deadline for proceedings:

　　3.1　One month before termination date specified in notice

　　3.2　Two weeks before termination date specified in notice

　　3.3　DEATH DATE for proceedings for new tenancy: termination date specified in notice

　　3.4　If an extension of time for proceedings to be issued is agreed, diarise corresponding dates running up to that deadline

Appendix 4

LANDLORD AND TENANT ACT 1954, PART II

LANDLORD AND TENANT ACT 1954, PART II

Security of Tenure for Business, Professional and other Tenants

Tenancies to which Part II applies

23 Tenancies to which Part II applies

(1)   Subject to the provisions of this Act, this Part of this Act applies to any tenancy where the property comprised in the tenancy is or includes premises which are occupied by the tenant and are so occupied for the purposes of a business carried on by him or for those and other purposes.

(1A)   Occupation or the carrying on of a business–

(a)   by a company in which the tenant has a controlling interest; or

(b)   where the tenant is a company, by a person with a controlling interest in the company,

shall be treated for the purposes of this section as equivalent to occupation or, as the case may be, the carrying on of a business by the tenant.

(1B)   Accordingly references (however expressed) in this Part of this Act to the business of, or to use, occupation or enjoyment by, the tenant shall be construed as including references to the business of, or to use, occupation or enjoyment by, a company falling within subsection (1A)(a) above or a person falling within subsection (1A)(b) above.

(2)   In this Part of this Act the expression 'business' includes a trade, profession or employment and includes any activity carried on by a body of persons, whether corporate or unincorporate.

(3)   In the following provisions of this Part of this Act the expression 'the holding', in relation to a tenancy to which this Part of this Act applies, means the property comprised in the tenancy, there being excluded any part thereof which is occupied neither by the tenant nor by a person employed by the tenant and so employed for the purposes of a business by reason of which the tenancy is one to which this Part of this Act applies.

(4)   Where the tenant is carrying on a business, in all or any part of the property comprised in a tenancy, in breach of a prohibition (however expressed) of use for business purposes which subsists under the terms of the tenancy and extends to the whole of that property, this Part of this Act shall not apply to the tenancy unless the immediate landlord or his predecessor in title has consented to the breach or the immediate landlord has acquiesced therein.

In this subsection the reference to a prohibition of use for business purposes does not include a prohibition of use for the purposes of a specified business, or of use for purposes of any but a specified business, but save as aforesaid includes a prohibition of use for the purposes of some one or more only of the classes of business specified in the definition of that expression in subsection (2) of this section.

Continuation and renewal of tenancies

24 Continuation of tenancies to which Part II applies and grant of new tenancies

(1)   A tenancy to which this Part of this Act applies shall not come to an end unless terminated in accordance with the provisions of this Part of this Act; and, subject to the following provisions of this Act either the tenant or the landlord under such a tenancy may apply to the court for an order for the grant of a new tenancy–

   (a) if the landlord has given notice under section 25 of this Act to terminate the tenancy, or

   (b) if the tenant has made a request for a new tenancy in accordance with section 26 of this Act.

(2)   The last foregoing subsection shall not prevent the coming to an end of a tenancy by notice to quit given by the tenant, by surrender or forfeiture, or by the forfeiture of a superior tenancy unless–

   (a) in the case of a notice to quit, the notice was given before the tenant had been in occupation in right of the tenancy for one month; . . .

   (b) . . .

(2A)   Neither the tenant nor the landlord may make an application under subsection (1) above if the other has made such an application and the application has been served.

(2B)   Neither the tenant nor the landlord may make such an application if the landlord has made an application under section 29(2) of this Act and the application has been served.

(2C)   The landlord may not withdraw an application under subsection (1) above unless the tenant consents to its withdrawal.

(3)   Notwithstanding anything in subsection (1) of this section–

   (a) where a tenancy to which this Part of this Act applies ceases to be such a tenancy, it shall not come to an end by reason only of the cesser, but if it was granted for a term of years certain and has been continued by subsection (1) of this section then (without prejudice to the termination thereof in accordance with any terms of the tenancy) it may be terminated by not less than three nor more than six months' notice in writing given by the landlord to the tenant;

   (b) where, at a time when a tenancy is not one to which this Part of this Act applies, the landlord gives notice to quit, the operation of the notice shall not be affected by reason that the tenancy becomes one to which this Part of this Act applies after the giving of the notice.

24A Applications for determination of interim rent while tenancy continues

(1)   Subject to subsection (2) below, if–

   (a) the landlord of a tenancy to which this Part of this Act applies has given notice under section 25 of this Act to terminate the tenancy; or

(b) the tenant of such a tenancy has made a request for a new tenancy in accordance with section 26 of this Act,

either of them may make an application to the court to determine a rent (an 'interim rent') which the tenant is to pay while the tenancy ('the relevant tenancy') continues by virtue of section 24 of this Act and the court may order payment of an interim rent in accordance with section 24C or 24D of this Act.

(2)   Neither the tenant nor the landlord may make an application under subsection (1) above if the other has made such an application and has not withdrawn it.

(3)   No application shall be entertained under subsection (1) above if it is made more than six months after the termination of the relevant tenancy.

24B Date from which interim rent is payable

(1)   The interim rent determined on an application under section 24A(1) of this Act shall be payable from the appropriate date.

(2)   If an application under section 24A(1) of this Act is made in a case where the landlord has given a notice under section 25 of this Act, the appropriate date is the earliest date of termination that could have been specified in the landlord's notice.

(3)   If an application under section 24A(1) of this Act is made in a case where the tenant has made a request for a new tenancy under section 26 of this Act, the appropriate date is the earliest date that could have been specified in the tenant's request as the date from which the new tenancy is to begin.

24C Amount of interim rent where new tenancy of whole premises granted and landlord not opposed

(1)   This section applies where–

(a) the landlord gave a notice under section 25 of this Act at a time when the tenant was in occupation of the whole of the property comprised in the relevant tenancy for purposes such as are mentioned in section 23(1) of this Act and stated in the notice that he was not opposed to the grant of a new tenancy; or

(b) the tenant made a request for a new tenancy under section 26 of this Act at a time when he was in occupation of the whole of that property for such purposes and the landlord did not give notice under subsection (6) of that section,

and the landlord grants a new tenancy of the whole of the property comprised in the relevant tenancy to the tenant (whether as a result of an order for the grant of a new tenancy or otherwise).

(2)   Subject to the following provisions of this section, the rent payable under and at the commencement of the new tenancy shall also be the interim rent.

(3)   Subsection (2) above does not apply where–

(a) the landlord or the tenant shows to the satisfaction of the court that the interim rent under that subsection differs substantially from the relevant rent; or

(b) the landlord or the tenant shows to the satisfaction of the court that the terms of the new tenancy differ from the terms of the relevant tenancy to such an extent that the interim rent under that subsection is substantially different from the rent which (in default of such agreement) the court would have determined under section 34 of this Act to be payable under a tenancy which commenced on the same day as the new tenancy and whose other terms were the same as the relevant tenancy.

(4)   In this section 'the relevant rent' means the rent which (in default of agreement between the landlord and the tenant) the court would have determined under section 34 of this Act to be payable under the new tenancy if the new tenancy had commenced on the appropriate date (within the meaning of section 24B of this Act).

(5)   The interim rent in a case where subsection (2) above does not apply by virtue only of subsection (3)(a) above is the relevant rent.

(6)   The interim rent in a case where subsection (2) above does not apply by virtue only of subsection (3)(b) above, or by virtue of subsection (3)(a) and (b) above, is the rent which it is reasonable for the tenant to pay while the relevant tenancy continues by virtue of section 24 of this Act.

(7)   In determining the interim rent under subsection (6) above the court shall have regard–

(a) to the rent payable under the terms of the relevant tenancy; and

(b) to the rent payable under any sub-tenancy of part of the property comprised in the relevant tenancy,

but otherwise subsections (1) and (2) of section 34 of this Act shall apply to the determination as they would apply to the determination of a rent under that section if a new tenancy of the whole of the property comprised in the relevant tenancy were granted to the tenant by order of the court and the duration of that new tenancy were the same as the duration of the new tenancy which is actually granted to the tenant.

(8)   In this section and section 24D of this Act 'the relevant tenancy' has the same meaning as in section 24A of this Act.

24D Amount of interim rent in any other case

(1)   The interim rent in a case where section 24C of this Act does not apply is the rent which it is reasonable for the tenant to pay while the relevant tenancy continues by virtue of section 24 of this Act.

(2)   In determining the interim rent under subsection (1) above the court shall have regard–

(a) to the rent payable under the terms of the relevant tenancy; and

(b) to the rent payable under any sub-tenancy of part of the property comprised in the relevant tenancy,

but otherwise subsections (1) and (2) of section 34 of this Act shall apply to the determination as they would apply to the determination of a rent under that section if a new tenancy from year to year of the whole of the property comprised in the relevant tenancy were granted to the tenant by order of the court.

(3)   If the court–

(a) has made an order for the grant of a new tenancy and has ordered payment of interim rent in accordance with section 24C of this Act, but

(b) either–

(i)   it subsequently revokes under section 36(2) of this Act the order for the grant of a new tenancy; or

(ii) the landlord and tenant agree not to act on the order,

the court on the application of the landlord or the tenant shall determine a new interim rent in accordance with subsections (1) and (2) above without a further application under section 24A(1) of this Act.

25 Termination of tenancy by the landlord

(1)   The landlord may terminate a tenancy to which this Part of this Act applies by a notice given to the tenant in the prescribed form specifying the date at which the tenancy is to come to an end (hereinafter referred to as 'the date of termination'):

Provided that this subsection has effect subject to the provisions of section 29B(4) of this Act and the provisions of Part IV of this Act as to the interim continuation of tenancies pending the disposal of applications to the court.

(2)   Subject to the provisions of the next following subsection, a notice under this section shall not have effect unless it is given not more than twelve nor less than six months before the date of termination specified therein.

(3)   In the case of a tenancy which apart from this Act could have been brought to an end by notice to quit given by the landlord–

(a) the date of termination specified in a notice under this section shall not be earlier than the earliest date on which apart from this Part of this Act the tenancy could have been brought to an end by notice to quit given by the landlord on the date of the giving of the notice under this section; and

(b) where apart from this Part of this Act more than six months' notice to quit would have been required to bring the tenancy to an end, the last foregoing subsection shall have effect with the substitution for twelve months of a period six months longer than the length of notice to quit which would have been required as aforesaid.

(4)   In the case of any other tenancy, a notice under this section shall not specify a date of termination earlier than the date on which apart from this Part of this Act the tenancy would have come to an end by effluxion of time.

(5)   . . .

(6)   A notice under this section shall not have effect unless it states whether the landlord is opposed to the grant of a new tenancy to the tenant.

(7)   A notice under this section which states that the landlord is opposed to the grant of a new tenancy to the tenant shall not have effect unless it also specifies one or more of the grounds specified in section 30(1) of this Act as the ground or grounds for his opposition.

(8)   A notice under this section which states that the landlord is not opposed to the grant of a new tenancy to the tenant shall not have effect unless it sets out the landlord's proposals as to–

(a)   the property to be comprised in the new tenancy (being either the whole or part of the property comprised in the current tenancy);

(b)   the rent to be payable under the new tenancy; and

(c)   the other terms of the new tenancy.

26 Tenant's request for a new tenancy

(1)   A tenant's request for a new tenancy may be made where the current tenancy is a tenancy granted for a term of years certain exceeding one year, whether or not continued by section 24 of this Act, or granted for a term of years certain and thereafter from year to year.

(2)   A tenant's request for a new tenancy shall be for a tenancy beginning with such date, not more than twelve nor less than six months after the making of the request, as may be specified therein:

Provided that the said date shall not be earlier than the date on which apart from this Act the current tenancy would come to an end by effluxion of time or could be brought to an end by notice to quit given by the tenant.

(3)   A tenant's request for a new tenancy shall not have effect unless it is made by notice in the prescribed form given to the landlord and sets out the tenant's proposals as to the property to be comprised in the new tenancy (being either the whole or part of the property comprised in the current tenancy), as to the rent to be payable under the new tenancy and as to the other terms of the new tenancy.

(4)   A tenant's request for a new tenancy shall not be made if the landlord has already given notice under the last foregoing section to terminate the current tenancy, or if the tenant has already given notice to quit or notice under the next following section; and no such notice shall be given by the landlord or the tenant after the making by the tenant of a request for a new tenancy.

(5)   Where the tenant makes a request for a new tenancy in accordance with the foregoing provisions of this section, the current tenancy shall, subject to the provisions of sections 29B(4) and 36(2) of this Act and the provisions of Part IV of this Act as to the interim continuation of tenancies, terminate immediately before the date specified in the request for the beginning of the new tenancy.

(6)   Within two months of the making of a tenant's request for a new tenancy the landlord may give notice to the tenant that he will oppose an application to the court for the grant of a new tenancy, and any such notice shall state on which of the grounds mentioned in section 30 of this Act the landlord will oppose the application.

27 Termination by tenant of tenancy for fixed term

(1)   Where the tenant under a tenancy to which this Part of this Act applies, being a tenancy granted for a term of years certain, gives to the immediate landlord, not later than three months before the date on which apart from this Act the tenancy would come to an end by effluxion of time, a notice in writing that the tenant does not desire the tenancy to be continued, section 24 of this Act shall not have effect in relation to the tenancy unless the notice is given before the tenant has been in occupation in right of the tenancy for one month.

(1A)   Section 24 of this Act shall not have effect in relation to a tenancy for a term of years certain where the tenant is not in occupation of the property comprised in the tenancy at the time when, apart from this Act, the tenancy would come to an end by effluxion of time.

(2)   A tenancy granted for a term of years certain which is continuing by virtue of section 24 of this Act shall not come to an end by reason only of the tenant ceasing to occupy the property comprised in the tenancy but may be brought to an end on any day by not less than three months' notice in writing given by the tenant to the immediate landlord, whether the notice is given after the date on which apart from this Act the tenancy would have come to an end or before that date, but not before the tenant has been in occupation in right of the tenancy for one month.

(3)   Where a tenancy is terminated under subsection (2) above, any rent payable in respect of a period which begins before, and ends after, the tenancy is terminated shall be apportioned, and any rent paid by the tenant in excess of the amount apportioned to the period before termination shall be recoverable by him.

28 Renewal of tenancies by agreement

Where the landlord and tenant agree for the grant to the tenant of a future tenancy of the holding, or of the holding with other land, on terms and from a date specified in the agreement, the current tenancy shall continue until that date but no longer, and shall not be a tenancy to which this Part of this Act applies.

Applications to court

29 Order by court for grant of new tenancy or termination of current tenancy

(1)   Subject to the provisions of this Act, on an application under section 24(1) of this Act, the court shall make an order for the grant of a new tenancy and accordingly for the termination of the current tenancy immediately before the commencement of the new tenancy.

(2)   Subject to the following provisions of this Act, a landlord may apply to the court for an order for the termination of a tenancy to which this Part of this Act applies without the grant of a new tenancy–

   (a)   if he has given notice under section 25 of this Act that he is opposed to the grant of a new tenancy to the tenant; or

(b) if the tenant has made a request for a new tenancy in accordance with section 26 of this Act and the landlord has given notice under subsection (6) of that section.

(3)   The landlord may not make an application under subsection (2) above if either the tenant or the landlord has made an application under section 24(1) of this Act.

(4)   Subject to the provisions of this Act, where the landlord makes an application under subsection (2) above–

(a) if he establishes, to the satisfaction of the court, any of the grounds on which he is entitled to make the application in accordance with section 30 of this Act, the court shall make an order for the termination of the current tenancy in accordance with section 64 of this Act without the grant of a new tenancy; and

(b) if not, it shall make an order for the grant of a new tenancy and accordingly for the termination of the current tenancy immediately before the commencement of the new tenancy.

(5)   The court shall dismiss an application by the landlord under section 24(1) of this Act if the tenant informs the court that he does not want a new tenancy.

(6)   The landlord may not withdraw an application under subsection (2) above unless the tenant consents to its withdrawal.

29A Time limits for applications to court

(1)   Subject to section 29B of this Act, the court shall not entertain an application–

(a) by the tenant or the landlord under section 24(1) of this Act; or

(b) by the landlord under section 29(2) of this Act,

if it is made after the end of the statutory period.

(2)   In this section and section 29B of this Act 'the statutory period' means a period ending–

(a) where the landlord gave a notice under section 25 of this Act, on the date specified in his notice; and

(b) where the tenant made a request for a new tenancy under section 26 of this Act, immediately before the date specified in his request.

(3)   Where the tenant has made a request for a new tenancy under section 26 of this Act, the court shall not entertain an application under section 24(1) of this Act which is made before the end of the period of two months beginning with the date of the making of the request, unless the application is made after the landlord has given a notice under section 26(6) of this Act.

29B Agreements extending time limits

(1)   After the landlord has given a notice under section 25 of this Act, or the tenant has made a request under section 26 of this Act, but before the end of the statutory period, the landlord and tenant may agree that an application such as is mentioned in section

29A(1) of this Act, may be made before the end of a period specified in the agreement which will expire after the end of the statutory period.

(2)   The landlord and tenant may from time to time by agreement further extend the period for making such an application, but any such agreement must be made before the end of the period specified in the current agreement.

(3)   Where an agreement is made under this section, the court may entertain an application such as is mentioned in section 29A(1) of this Act if it is made before the end of the period specified in the agreement.

(4)   Where an agreement is made under this section, or two or more agreements are made under this section, the landlord's notice under section 25 of this Act or tenant's request under section 26 of this Act shall be treated as terminating the tenancy at the end of the period specified in the agreement or, as the case may be, at the end of the period specified in the last of those agreements.

30 Opposition by landlord to application for a new tenancy

(1)   The grounds on which a landlord may oppose an application under section 24(1) of this Act, or make an application under section 29(2) of this Act, are such of the following grounds as may be stated in the landlord's notice under section 25 of this Act or, as the case may be, under subsection (6) of section 26 thereof, that is to say:–

(a) where under the current tenancy the tenant has any obligations as respects the repair and maintenance of the holding, that the tenant ought not to be granted a new tenancy in view of the state of repair of the holding, being a state resulting from the tenant's failure to comply with the said obligations;

(b) that the tenant ought not to be granted a new tenancy in view of his persistent delay in paying rent which has become due;

(c) that the tenant ought not to be granted a new tenancy in view of other substantial breaches by him of his obligations under the current tenancy, or for any other reason connected with the tenant's use or management of the holding;

(d) that the landlord has offered and is willing to provide or secure the provision of alternative accommodation for the tenant, that the terms on which the alternative accommodation is available are reasonable having regard to the terms of the current tenancy and to all other relevant circumstances, and that the accommodation and the time at which it will be available are suitable for the tenant's requirements (including the requirement to preserve goodwill) having regard to the nature and class of his business and to the situation and extent of, and facilities afforded by, the holding;

(e) where the current tenancy was created by the sub-letting of part only of the property comprised in a superior tenancy and the landlord is the owner of an interest in reversion expectant on the termination of that superior tenancy, that the aggregate of the rents reasonably obtainable on separate lettings of the holding and the remainder of that property would be substantially less than the rent reasonably obtainable on a letting of that property as a whole, that on the termination of the current tenancy the landlord requires possession of the holding for the purpose of letting or otherwise disposing of the said property as a whole, and that in view thereof the tenant ought not to be granted a new tenancy;

(f) that on the termination of the current tenancy the landlord intends to demolish or reconstruct the premises comprised in the holding or a substantial part of those premises or to carry out substantial work of construction on the holding or part thereof and that he could not reasonably do so without obtaining possession of the holding;

(g) subject as hereinafter provided, that on the termination of the current tenancy the landlord intends to occupy the holding for the purposes, or partly for the purposes, of a business to be carried on by him therein, or as his residence.

(1A)   Where the landlord has a controlling interest in a company, the reference in subsection (1)(g) above to the landlord shall be construed as a reference to the landlord or that company.

(1B)   Subject to subsection (2A) below, where the landlord is a company and a person has a controlling interest in the company, the reference in subsection (1)(g) above to the landlord shall be construed as a reference to the landlord or that person.

(2)   The landlord shall not be entitled to oppose an application under section 24(1) of this Act, or make an application under section 29(2) of this Act, on the ground specified in paragraph (g) of the last foregoing subsection if the interest of the landlord, or an interest which has merged in that interest and but for the merger would be the interest of the landlord, was purchased or created after the beginning of the period of five years which ends with the termination of the current tenancy, and at all times since the purchase or creation thereof the holding has been comprised in a tenancy or successive tenancies of the description specified in subsection (1) of section 23 of this Act.

(2A)   Subsection (1B) above shall not apply if the controlling interest was acquired after the beginning of the period of five years which ends with the termination of the current tenancy, and at all times since the acquisition of the controlling interest the holding has been comprised in a tenancy or successive tenancies of the description specified in section 23(1) of this Act.

(3)   . . .

31 Dismissal of application for new tenancy where landlord successfully opposes

(1)   If the landlord opposes an application under subsection (1) of section 24 of this Act on grounds on which he is entitled to oppose it in accordance with the last foregoing section and establishes any of those grounds to the satisfaction of the court, the court shall not make an order for the grant of a new tenancy.

(2)   Where the landlord opposes an application under section 24(1) of this Act, or makes an application under section 29(2) of this Act, on one or more of the grounds specified in section 30(1)(d) to (f) of this Act but establishes none of those grounds, and none of the other grounds specified in section 30(1) of this Act, to the satisfaction of the court, then if the court would have been satisfied on any of the grounds specified in section 30(1)(d) to (f) of this Act if the date of termination specified in the landlord's

notice or, as the case may be, the date specified in the tenant's request for a new tenancy as the date from which the new tenancy is to begin, had been such later date as the court may determine, being a date not more than one year later than the date so specified,–

(a) the court shall make a declaration to that effect, stating of which of the said grounds the court would have been satisfied as aforesaid and specifying the date determined by the court as aforesaid, but shall not make an order for the grant of a new tenancy;

(b) if, within fourteen days after the making of the declaration, the tenant so requires the court shall make an order substituting the said date for the date specified in the said landlord's notice or tenant's request, and thereupon that notice or request shall have effect accordingly.

31A Grant of new tenancy in some cases where section 30(1)(f) applies

(1) Where the landlord opposes an application under section 24(1) of this Act on the ground specified in paragraph (f) of section 30(1) of this Act, or makes an application under section 29(2) of this Act on that ground, the court shall not hold that the landlord could not reasonably carry out the demolition, reconstruction or work of construction intended without obtaining possession of the holding if–

(a) the tenant agrees to the inclusion in the terms of the new tenancy of terms giving the landlord access and other facilities for carrying out the work intended and, given that access and those facilities, the landlord could reasonably carry out the work without obtaining possession of the holding and without interfering to a substantial extent or for a substantial time with the use of the holding for the purposes of the business carried on by the tenant; or

(b) the tenant is willing to accept a tenancy of an economically separable part of the holding and either paragraph (a) of this section is satisfied with respect to that part or possession of the remainder of the holding would be reasonably sufficient to enable the landlord to carry out the intended work.

(2) For the purposes of subsection (1)(b) of this section a part of a holding shall be deemed to be an economically separable part if, and only if, the aggregate of the rents which, after the completion of the intended work, would be reasonably obtainable on separate lettings of that part and the remainder of the premises affected by or resulting from the work would not be substantially less than the rent which would then be reasonably obtainable on a letting of those premises as a whole.

32 Property to be comprised in new tenancy

(1) Subject to the following provisions of this section, an order under section 29 of this Act for the grant of a new tenancy shall be an order for the grant of a new tenancy of the holding; and in the absence of agreement between the landlord and the tenant as to the property which constitutes the holding the court shall in the order designate that property by reference to the circumstances existing at the date of the order.

(1A) Where the court, by virtue of paragraph (b) of section 31A(1) of this Act, makes an order under section 29 of this Act for the grant of a new tenancy in a case where the tenant is willing to accept a tenancy of part of the holding, the order shall be an order for the grant of a new tenancy of that part only.

(2)   The foregoing provisions of this section shall not apply in a case where the property comprised in the current tenancy includes other property besides the holding and the landlord requires any new tenancy ordered to be granted under section 29 of this Act to be a tenancy of the whole of the property comprised in the current tenancy; but in any such case–

(a)   any order under the said section 29 for the grant of a new tenancy shall be an order for the grant of a new tenancy of the whole of the property comprised in the current tenancy, and

(b)   references in the following provisions of this Part of this Act to the holding shall be construed as references to the whole of that property.

(3)   Where the current tenancy includes rights enjoyed by the tenant in connection with the holding, those rights shall be included in a tenancy ordered to be granted under section 29 of this Act except as otherwise agreed between the landlord and the tenant or, in default of such agreement, determined by the court.

33 Duration of new tenancy

Where on an application under this Part of this Act the court makes an order for the grant of a new tenancy, the new tenancy shall be such tenancy as may be agreed between the landlord and the tenant, or, in default of such an agreement, shall be such a tenancy as may be determined by the court to be reasonable in all the circumstances, being, if it is a tenancy for a term of years certain, a tenancy for a term not exceeding fifteen years, and shall begin on the coming to an end of the current tenancy.

34 Rent under new tenancy

(1)   The rent payable under a tenancy granted by order of the court under this Part of this Act shall be such as may be agreed between the landlord and the tenant or as, in default of such agreement, may be determined by the court to be that at which, having regard to the terms of the tenancy (other than those relating to rent), the holding might reasonably be expected to be let in the open market by a willing lessor, there being disregarded–

(a)   any effect on rent of the fact that the tenant has or his predecessors in title have been in occupation of the holding,

(b)   any goodwill attached to the holding by reason of the carrying on thereat of the business of the tenant (whether by him or by a predecessor of his in that business),

(c)   any effect on rent of an improvement to which this paragraph applies,

(d)   in the case of a holding comprising licensed premises, any addition to its value attributable to the licence, if it appears to the court that having regard to the terms of the current tenancy and any other relevant circumstances the benefit of the licence belongs to the tenant.

(2)   Paragraph (c) of the foregoing subsection applies to any improvement carried out by a person who at the time it was carried out was the tenant, but only if it was carried out otherwise than in pursuance of an obligation to his immediate landlord, and either it was carried out during the current tenancy or the following conditions are satisfied, that is to say–

(a)   that it was completed not more than twenty-one years before the application to the court was made; and

(b)   that the holding or any part of it affected by the improvement has at all times since the completion of the improvement been comprised in tenancies of the description specified in section 23(1) of this Act; and

(c)   that at the termination of each of those tenancies the tenant did not quit.

(2A)   If this Part of this Act applies by virtue of section 23(1A) of this Act, the reference in subsection (1)(d) above to the tenant shall be construed as including–

(a)   a company in which the tenant has a controlling interest, or

(b)   where the tenant is a company, a person with a controlling interest in the company.

(3)   Where the rent is determined by the court the court may, if it thinks fit, further determine that the terms of the tenancy shall include such provision for varying the rent as may be specified in the determination.

(4)   It is hereby declared that the matters which are to be taken into account by the court in determining the rent include any effect on rent of the operation of the provisions of the Landlord and Tenant (Covenants) Act 1995.

35 Other terms of new tenancy

(1)   The terms of a tenancy granted by order of the court under this Part of this Act (other than terms as to the duration thereof and as to the rent payable thereunder), including, where different persons own interests which fulfil the conditions specified in section 44(1) of this Act in different parts of it, terms as to the apportionment of the rent, shall be such as may be agreed between the landlord and the tenant or as, in default of such agreement, may be determined by the court; and in determining those terms the court shall have regard to the terms of the current tenancy and to all relevant circumstances.

(2)   In subsection (1) of this section the reference to all relevant circumstances includes (without prejudice to the generality of that reference) a reference to the operation of the provisions of the Landlord and Tenant (Covenants) Act 1995.

36 Carrying out of order for new tenancy

(1)   Where under this Part of this Act the court makes an order for the grant of a new tenancy, then, unless the order is revoked under the next following subsection or the landlord and the tenant agree not to act upon the order, the landlord shall be bound to execute or make in favour of the tenant, and the tenant shall be bound to accept, a lease

or agreement for a tenancy of the holding embodying the terms agreed between the landlord and the tenant or determined by the court in accordance with the foregoing provisions of this Part of this Act; and where the landlord executes or makes such a lease or agreement the tenant shall be bound, if so required by the landlord, to execute a counterpart or duplicate thereof.

(2)   If the tenant, within fourteen days after the making of an order under this Part of this Act for the grant of a new tenancy, applies to the court for the revocation of the order the court shall revoke the order; and where the order is so revoked, then, if it is so agreed between the landlord and the tenant or determined by the court, the current tenancy shall continue, beyond the date at which it would have come to an end apart from this subsection, for such period as may be so agreed or determined to be necessary to afford to the landlord a reasonable opportunity for reletting or otherwise disposing of the premises which would have been comprised in the new tenancy; and while the current tenancy continues by virtue of this subsection it shall not be a tenancy to which this Part of this Act applies.

(3)   Where an order is revoked under the last foregoing subsection any provision thereof as to payment of costs shall not cease to have effect by reason only of the revocation; but the court may, if it thinks fit, revoke or vary any such provision or, where no costs have been awarded in the proceedings for the revoked order, award such costs.

(4)   A lease executed or agreement made under this section, in a case where the interest of the lessor is subject to a mortgage, shall be deemed to be one authorised by section 99 of the Law of Property Act 1925 (which confers certain powers of leasing on mortgagors in possession), and subsection (13) of that section (which allows those powers to be restricted or excluded by agreement) shall not have effect in relation to such a lease or agreement.

37 Compensation where order for new tenancy precluded on certain grounds

(1)   Subject to the provisions of this Act, in a case specified in subsection (1A), (1B) or (1C) below (a 'compensation case') the tenant shall be entitled on quitting the holding to recover from the landlord by way of compensation an amount determined in accordance with this section.

(1A)   The first compensation case is where on the making of an application by the tenant under section 24(1) of this Act the court is precluded (whether by subsection (1) or subsection (2) of section 31 of this Act) from making an order for the grant of a new tenancy by reason of any of the grounds specified in paragraphs (e), (f) and (g) of section 30(1) of this Act (the 'compensation grounds') and not of any grounds specified in any other paragraph of section 30(1).

(1B)   The second compensation case is where on the making of an application under section 29(2) of this Act the court is precluded (whether by section 29(4)(a) or section 31(2) of this Act) from making an order for the grant of a new tenancy by reason of any of the compensation grounds and not of any other grounds specified in section 30(1) of this Act.

(1C)   The third compensation case is where–

(a) the landlord's notice under section 25 of this Act or, as the case may be, under section 26(6) of this Act, states his opposition to the grant of a new tenancy on any of the compensation grounds and not on any other grounds specified in section 30(1) of this Act; and

(b) either–

   (i)   no application is made by the tenant under section 24(1) of this Act or by the landlord under section 29(2) of this Act; or

   (ii)   such an application is made but is subsequently withdrawn.

(2)   Subject to the following provisions of this section, compensation under this section shall be as follows, that is to say–

(a) where the conditions specified in the next following subsection are satisfied in relation to the whole of the holding it shall be the product of the appropriate multiplier and twice the rateable value of the holding,

(b) in any other case it shall be the product of the appropriate multiplier and the rateable value of the holding.

(3)   The said conditions are–

(a) that, during the whole of the fourteen years immediately preceding the termination of the current tenancy, premises being or comprised in the holding have been occupied for the purposes of a business carried on by the occupier or for those and other purposes;

(b) that, if during those fourteen years there was a change in the occupier of the premises, the person who was the occupier immediately after the change was the successor to the business carried on by the person who was the occupier immediately before the change.

(3A)   If the conditions specified in subsection (3) above are satisfied in relation to part of the holding but not in relation to the other part, the amount of compensation shall be the aggregate of sums calculated separately as compensation in respect of each part, and accordingly, for the purpose of calculating compensation in respect of a part any reference in this section to the holding shall be construed as a reference to that part.

(3B)   Where section 44(1A) of this Act applies, the compensation shall be determined separately for each part and compensation determined for any part shall be recoverable only from the person who is the owner of an interest in that part which fulfils the conditions specified in section 44(1) of this Act.

(4)   Where the court is precluded from making an order for the grant of a new tenancy under this Part of this Act in a compensation case, the court shall on the application of the tenant certify that fact.

(5)   For the purposes of subsection (2) of this section the rateable value of the holding shall be determined as follows:–

(a) where in the valuation list in force at the date on which the landlord's notice under section 25 or, as the case may be, subsection (6) of section 26 of this Act is given a value is then shown as the annual value (as hereinafter defined) of the holding, the rateable value of the holding shall be taken to be that value;

(b) where no such value is so shown with respect to the holding but such a value or such values is or are so shown with respect to premises comprised in or comprising the holding or part of it, the rateable value of the holding shall be taken to be such value as is found by a proper apportionment or aggregation of the value or values so shown;

(c) where the rateable value of the holding cannot be ascertained in accordance with the foregoing paragraphs of this subsection, it shall be taken to be the value which, apart from any exemption from assessment to rates, would on a proper assessment be the value to be entered in the said valuation list as the annual value of the holding;

and any dispute arising, whether in proceedings before the court or otherwise, as to the determination for those purposes of the rateable value of the holding shall be referred to the Commissioners of Inland Revenue for decision by a valuation officer.

An appeal shall lie to the Lands Tribunal from any decision of a valuation officer under this subsection, but subject thereto any such decision shall be final.

(5A)   If part of the holding is domestic property, as defined in section 66 of the Local Government Finance Act 1988–

(a) the domestic property shall be disregarded in determining the rateable value of the holding under subsection (5) of this section; and

(b) if, on the date specified in subsection (5) (a) of this section, the tenant occupied the whole or any part of the domestic property, the amount of compensation to which he is entitled under subsection (1) of this section shall be increased by the addition of a sum equal to his reasonable expenses in removing from the domestic property.

(5B)   Any question as to the amount of the sum referred to in paragraph (b) of subsection (5A) of this section shall be determined by agreement between the landlord and the tenant or, in default of agreement, by the court.

(5C)   If the whole of the holding is domestic property, as defined in section 66 of the Local Government Finance Act 1988, for the purposes of subsection (2) of this section the rateable value of the holding shall be taken to be an amount equal to the rent at which it is estimated the holding might reasonably be expected to let from year to year if the tenant undertook to pay all usual tenant's rates and taxes and to bear the cost of the repairs and insurance and the other expenses (if any) necessary to maintain the holding in a state to command that rent.

(5D)   The following provisions shall have effect as regards a determination of an amount mentioned in subsection (5C) of this section–

(a) the date by reference to which such a determination is to be made is the date on which the landlord's notice under section 25 or, as the case may be, subsection (6) of section 26 of this Act is given;

(b) any dispute arising, whether in proceedings before the court or otherwise, as to such a determination shall be referred to the Commissioners of Inland Revenue for decision by a valuation officer;

(c) an appeal shall lie to the Lands Tribunal from such a decision but subject to that, such a decision shall be final.

(5E) Any deduction made under paragraph 2A of Schedule 6 to the Local Government Finance Act 1988 (deduction from valuation of hereditaments used for breeding horses etc) shall be disregarded, to the extent that it relates to the holding, in determining the rateable value of the holding under subsection (5) of this section.

(6) The Commissioners of Inland Revenue may by statutory instrument make rules prescribing the procedure in connection with references under this section.

(7) In this section–

the reference to the termination of the current tenancy is a reference to the date of termination specified in the landlord's notice under section 25 of this Act or, as the case may be, the date specified in the tenant's request for a new tenancy as the date from which the new tenancy is to begin;

the expression 'annual value' means rateable value except that where the rateable value differs from the net annual value the said expression means net annual value;

the expression 'valuation officer' means any officer of the Commissioners of Inland Revenue for the time being authorised by a certificate of the Commissioners to act in relation to a valuation list.

(8) In subsection (2) of this section 'the appropriate multiplier' means such multiplier as the Secretary of State may by order made by statutory instrument prescribe and different multipliers may be so prescribed in relation to different cases.

(9) A statutory instrument containing an order under subsection (8) of this section shall be subject to annulment in pursuance of a resolution of either House of Parliament.

37A Compensation for possession obtained by misrepresentation

(1) Where the court–

(a) makes an order for the termination of the current tenancy but does not make an order for the grant of a new tenancy, or

(b) refuses an order for the grant of a new tenancy,

and it subsequently made to appear to the court that the order was obtained, or the court was induced to refuse the grant, by misrepresentation or the concealment of material facts, the court may order the landlord to pay to the tenant such sum as appears sufficient as compensation for damage or loss sustained by the tenant as the result of the order or refusal.

(2) Where–

(a) the tenant has quit the holding–

(i) after making but withdrawing an application under section 24(1) of this Act; or

(ii) without making such an application; and

(b) it is made to appear to the court that he did so by reason of misrepresentation or the concealment of material facts,

the court may order the landlord to pay to the tenant such sum as appears sufficient as compensation for damage or loss sustained by the tenant as the result of quitting the holding.

38 Restriction on agreements excluding provisions of Part II

(1) Any agreement relating to a tenancy to which this Part of this Act applies (whether contained in the instrument creating the tenancy or not) shall be void (except as provided by section 38A of this Act) in so far as it purports to preclude the tenant from making an application or request under this Part of this Act or provides for the termination or the surrender of the tenancy in the event of his making such an application or request or for the imposition of any penalty or disability on the tenant in that event.

(2) Where–

(a) during the whole of the five years immediately preceding the date on which the tenant under a tenancy to which this Part of this Act applies is to quit the holding, premises being or comprised in the holding have been occupied for the purposes of a business carried on by the occupier or for those and other purposes, and

(b) if during those five years there was a change in the occupier of the premises, the person who was the occupier immediately after the change was the successor to the business carried on by the person who was the occupier immediately before the change,

any agreement (whether contained in the instrument creating the tenancy or not and whether made before or after the termination of that tenancy) which purports to exclude or reduce compensation under section 37 of this Act shall to that extent be void, so however that this subsection shall not affect any agreement as to the amount of any such compensation which is made after the right to compensation has accrued.

(3) In a case not falling within the last foregoing subsection the right to compensation conferred by section 37 of this Act may be excluded or modified by agreement.

(4) . . .

38A Agreements to exclude provisions of Part II

(1) The persons who will be the landlord and the tenant in relation to a tenancy to be granted for a term of years certain which will be a tenancy to which this Part of this Act applies may agree that the provisions of sections 24 to 28 of this Act shall be excluded in relation to that tenancy.

(2) The persons who are the landlord and the tenant in relation to a tenancy to which this Part of this Act applies may agree that the tenancy shall be surrendered on such date or in such circumstances as may be specified in the agreement and on such terms (if any) as may be so specified.

(3) An agreement under subsection (1) above shall be void unless–

(a) the landlord has served on the tenant a notice in the form, or substantially in the form, set out in Schedule 1 to the Regulatory Reform (Business Tenancies) (England and Wales) Order 2003 ('the 2003 Order'); and

(b) the requirements specified in Schedule 2 to that Order are met.

(4)   An agreement under subsection (2) above shall be void unless–

(a) the landlord has served on the tenant a notice in the form, or substantially in the form, set out in Schedule 3 to the 2003 Order; and

(b) the requirements specified in Schedule 4 to that Order are met.

General and supplementary provisions

39 Saving for compulsory acquisitions

(1)   . . .

(2)   If the amount of the compensation which would have been payable under section 37 of this Act if the tenancy had come to an end in circumstances giving rise to compensation under that section and the date at which the acquiring authority obtained possession had been the termination of the current tenancy exceeds the amount of the compensation payable under section 121 of the Lands Clauses Consolidation Act 1845 or section 20 of the Compulsory Purchase Act 1965 in the case of a tenancy to which this Part of this Act applies, that compensation shall be increased by the amount of the excess.

(3)   Nothing in section 24 of this Act shall affect the operation of the said section 121.

40 Duties of tenants and landlords of business premises to give information to each other

(1)   Where a person who is an owner of an interest in reversion expectant (whether immediately or not) on a tenancy of any business premises has served on the tenant a notice in the prescribed form requiring him to do so, it shall be the duty of the tenant to give the appropriate person in writing the information specified in subsection (2) below.

(2)   That information is–

(a) whether the tenant occupies the premises or any part of them wholly or partly for the purposes of a business carried on by him;

(b) whether his tenancy has effect subject to any sub-tenancy on which his tenancy is immediately expectant and, if so–

(i)   what premises are comprised in the sub-tenancy;

(ii) for what term it has effect (or, if it is terminable by notice, by what notice it can be terminated);

(iii) what is the rent payable under it;

(iv) who is the sub-tenant;

(v) (to the best of his knowledge and belief) whether the sub-tenant is in occupation of the premises or of part of the premises comprised in the sub-tenancy and, if not, what is the sub-tenant's address;

(vi) whether an agreement is in force excluding in relation to the sub-tenancy the provisions of sections 24 to 28 of this Act; and

(vii) whether a notice has been given under section 25 or 26(6) of this Act, or a request has been made under section 26 of this Act, in relation to the sub-tenancy and, if so, details of the notice or request; and

(c) (to the best of his knowledge and belief) the name and address of any other person who owns an interest in reversion in any part of the premises.

(3)   Where the tenant of any business premises who is a tenant under such a tenancy as is mentioned in section 26(1) of this Act has served on a reversioner or a reversioner's mortgagee in possession a notice in the prescribed form requiring him to do so, it shall be the duty of the person on whom the notice is served to give the appropriate person in writing the information specified in subsection (4) below.

(4)   That information is–

(a) whether he is the owner of the fee simple in respect of the premises or any part of them or the mortgagee in possession of such an owner,

(b) if he is not, then (to the best of his knowledge and belief)–

(i) the name and address of the person who is his or, as the case may be, his mortgagor's immediate landlord in respect of those premises or of the part in respect of which he or his mortgagor is not the owner in fee simple;

(ii) for what term his or his mortgagor's tenancy has effect and what is the earliest date (if any) at which that tenancy is terminable by notice to quit given by the landlord; and

(iii) whether a notice has been given under section 25 or 26(6) of this Act, or a request has been made under section 26 of this Act, in relation to the tenancy and, if so, details of the notice or request;

(c) (to the best of his knowledge and belief) the name and address of any other person who owns an interest in reversion in any part of the premises; and

(d) if he is a reversioner, whether there is a mortgagee in possession of his interest in the premises and, if so, (to the best of his knowledge and belief) what is the name and address of the mortgagee.

(5)   A duty imposed on a person by this section is a duty–

(a) to give the information concerned within the period of one month beginning with the date of service of the notice; and

(b) if within the period of six months beginning with the date of service of the notice that person becomes aware that any information which has been given in pursuance of the notice is not, or is no longer, correct, to give the appropriate person correct information within the period of one month beginning with the date on which he becomes aware.

(6) This section shall not apply to a notice served by or on the tenant more than two years before the date on which apart from this Act his tenancy would come to an end by effluxion of time or could be brought to an end by notice to quit given by the landlord.

(7) Except as provided by section 40A of this Act, the appropriate person for the purposes of this section and section 40A(1) of this Act is the person who served the notice under subsection (1) or (3) above.

(8) In this section–

'business premises' means premises used wholly or partly for the purposes of a business;

'mortgagee in possession' includes a receiver appointed by the mortgagee or by the court who is in receipt of the rents and profits, and 'his mortgagor' shall be construed accordingly;

'reversioner' means any person having an interest in the premises, being an interest in reversion expectant (whether immediately or not) on the tenancy;

'reversioner's mortgagee in possession' means any person being a mortgagee in possession in respect of such an interest; and

'sub-tenant' includes a person retaining possession of any premises by virtue of the Rent (Agriculture) Act 1976 or the Rent Act 1977 after the coming to an end of a sub-tenancy, and 'sub-tenancy' includes a right so to retain possession.

40A Duties in transfer cases

(1) If a person on whom a notice under section 40(1) or (3) of this Act has been served has transferred his interest in the premises or any part of them to some other person and gives the appropriate person notice in writing–

(a) of the transfer of his interest; and

(b) of the name and address of the person to whom he transferred it,

on giving the notice he ceases in relation to the premises or (as the case may be) to that part to be under any duty imposed by section 40 of this Act.

(2) If–

(a) the person who served the notice under section 40(1) or (3) of this Act ('the transferor') has transferred his interest in the premises to some other person ('the transferee'); and

(b) the transferor or the transferee has given the person required to give the information notice in writing–

(i) of the transfer; and

(ii) of the transferee's name and address,

the appropriate person for the purposes of section 40 of this Act and subsection (1) above is the transferee.

(3)   If–

(a) a transfer such as is mentioned in paragraph (a) of subsection (2) above has taken place; but

(b) neither the transferor nor the transferee has given a notice such as is mentioned in paragraph (b) of that subsection,

any duty imposed by section 40 of this Act may be performed by giving the information either to the transferor or to the transferee.

40B Proceedings for breach of duties to give information

A claim that a person has broken any duty imposed by section 40 of this Act may be made the subject of civil proceedings for breach of statutory duty; and in any such proceedings a court may order that person to comply with that duty and may make an award of damages.

41 Trusts

(1)   Where a tenancy is held on trust, occupation by all or any of the beneficiaries under the trust, and the carrying on of a business by all or any of the beneficiaries, shall be treated for the purposes of section 23 of this Act as equivalent to occupation or the carrying on of a business by the tenant; and in relation to a tenancy to which this Part of this Act applies by virtue of the foregoing provisions of this subsection–

(a) references (however expressed) in this Part of this Act and in the Ninth Schedule to this Act to the business of, or to carrying on of business, use, occupation or enjoyment by, the tenant shall be construed as including references to the business of, or to carrying on of business, use, occupation or enjoyment by, the beneficiaries or beneficiary;

(b) the reference in paragraph (d) of subsection (1) of section 34 of this Act to the tenant shall be construed as including the beneficiaries or beneficiary; and

(c) a change in the persons of the trustees shall not be treated as a change in the person of the tenant.

(2)   Where the landlord's interest is held on trust the references in paragraph (g) of subsection (1) of section 30 of this Act to the landlord shall be construed as including references to the beneficiaries under the trust or any of them; but, except in the case of a trust arising under a will or on the intestacy of any person, the reference in subsection (2) of that section to the creation of the interest therein mentioned shall be construed as including the creation of the trust.

41A Partnerships

(1)   The following provisions of this section shall apply where–

(a) a tenancy is held jointly by two or more persons (in this section referred to as the joint tenants); and

(b) the property comprised in the tenancy is or includes premises occupied for the purposes of a business; and

(c) the business (or some other business) was at some time during the existence of the tenancy carried on in partnership by all the persons who were then the joint tenants or by those and other persons and the joint tenants' interest in the premises was then partnership property; and

(d) the business is carried on (whether alone or in partnership with other persons) by one or some only of the joint tenants and no part of the property comprised in the tenancy is occupied, in right of the tenancy, for the purposes of a business carried on (whether alone or in partnership with other persons) by the other or others.

(2)   In the following provisions of this section those of the joint tenants who for the time being carry on the business are referred to as the business tenants and the others as the other joint tenants.

(3)   Any notice given by the business tenants which, had it been given by all the joint tenants, would have been–

(a) a tenant's request for a new tenancy made in accordance with section 26 of this Act; or

(b) a notice under subsection (1) or subsection (2) of section 27 of this Act;

shall be treated as such if it states that it is given by virtue of this section and sets out the facts by virtue of which the persons giving it are the business tenants; and references in those sections and in section 24A of this Act to the tenant shall be construed accordingly.

(4)   A notice given by the landlord to the business tenants which, had it been given to all the joint tenants, would have been a notice under section 25 of this Act shall be treated as such a notice, and references in that section to the tenant shall be construed accordingly.

(5)   An application under section 24(1) of this Act for a new tenancy may, instead of being made by all the joint tenants, be made by the business tenants alone; and where it is so made–

(a) this Part of this Act shall have effect, in relation to it, as if the references therein to the tenant included references to the business tenants alone; and

(b) the business tenants shall be liable, to the exclusion of the other joint tenants, for the payment of rent and the discharge of any other obligation under the current tenancy for any rental period beginning after the date specified in the landlord's notice under section 25 of this Act or, as the case may be, beginning on or after the date specified in their request for a new tenancy.

(6)   Where the court makes an order under section 29 of this Act for the grant of a new tenancy it may order the grant to be made to the business tenants or to them jointly with the persons carrying on the business in partnership with them, and may order the grant to be made subject to the satisfaction, within a time specified by the order, of such conditions as to guarantors, sureties or otherwise as appear to the court equitable, having regard to the omission of the other joint tenants from the persons who will be the tenant under the new tenancy.

(7)   The business tenants shall be entitled to recover any amount payable by way of compensation under section 37 or section 59 of this Act.

42 Groups of companies

(1)   For the purposes of this section two bodies corporate shall be taken to be members of a group if and only if one is a subsidiary of the other or both are subsidiaries of a third body corporate or the same person has a controlling interest in both.

(2)   Where a tenancy is held by a member of a group, occupation by another member of the group, and the carrying on of a business by another member of the group, shall be treated for the purposes of section 23 of this Act as equivalent to occupation or the carrying on of a business by the member of the group holding the tenancy; and in relation to a tenancy to which this Part of this Act applies by virtue of the foregoing provisions of this subsection–

-   (a)   references (however expressed) in this Part of this Act and in the Ninth Schedule to this Act to the business of or to use occupation or enjoyment by the tenant shall be construed as including references to the business of or to use occupation or enjoyment by the said other member;

-   (b)   the reference in paragraph (d) of subsection (1) of section 34 of this Act to the tenant shall be construed as including the said other member; and

-   (c)   an assignment of the tenancy from one member of the group to another shall not be treated as a change in the person of the tenant.

(3)   Where the landlord's interest is held by a member of a group–

-   (a)   the reference in paragraph (g) of subsection (1) of section 30 of this Act to intended occupation by the landlord for the purposes of a business to be carried on by him shall be construed as including intended occupation by any member of the group for the purposes of a business to be carried on by that member; and

-   (b)   the reference in subsection (2) of that section to the purchase or creation of any interest shall be construed as a reference to a purchase from or creation by a person other than a member of the group.

43 Tenancies excluded from Part II

(1)   This Part of this Act does not apply–

-   (a)   to a tenancy of an agricultural holding which is a tenancy in relation to which the Agricultural Holdings Act 1986 applies or a tenancy which would be a tenancy of an agricultural holding in relation to which that Act applied if subsection (3) of section 2 of that Act did not have effect or, in a case where approval was given under subsection (1) of that section, if that approval had not been given;

-   (aa) to a farm business tenancy;

-   (b)   to a tenancy created by a mining lease; . . .

        . . .

(2)   This Part of this Act does not apply to a tenancy granted by reason that the tenant was the holder of an office, appointment or employment from the grantor thereof and continuing only so long as the tenant holds the office, appointment or employment, or terminable by the grantor on the tenant's ceasing to hold it, or coming to an end at a time fixed by reference to the time at which the tenant ceases to hold it:

Provided that this subsection shall not have effect in relation to a tenancy granted after the commencement of this Act unless the tenancy was granted by an instrument in writing which expressed the purpose for which the tenancy was granted.

(3)   This Part of this Act does not apply to a tenancy granted for a term certain not exceeding six months unless–

   (a) the tenancy contains provision for renewing the term or for extending it beyond six months from its beginning; or

   (b) the tenant has been in occupation for a period which, together with any period during which any predecessor in the carrying on of the business carried on by the tenant was in occupation, exceeds twelve months.

43A Jurisdiction of county court to make declaration

Where the rateable value of the holding is such that the jurisdiction conferred on the court by any other provision of this Part of this Act is, by virtue of section 63 of this Act, exercisable by the county court, the county court shall have jurisdiction (but without prejudice to the jurisdiction of the High Court) to make any declaration as to any matter arising under this Part of this Act, whether or not any other relief is sought in the proceedings.

44 Meaning of 'the landlord' in Part II, and provisions as to mesne landlords, etc.

(1)   Subject to subsections (1A) and (2) below, in this Part of this Act the expression 'the landlord', in relation to a tenancy (in this section referred to as 'the relevant tenancy'), means the person (whether or not he is the immediate landlord) who is the owner of that interest in the property comprised in the relevant tenancy which for the time being fulfils the following conditions, that is to say–

   (a) that it is an interest in reversion expectant (whether immediately or not) on the termination of the relevant tenancy, and

   (b) that it is either the fee simple or a tenancy which will not come to an end within fourteen months by effluxion of time and, if it is such a tenancy, that no notice has been given by virtue of which it will come to an end within fourteen months or any further time by which it may be continued under section 36(2) or section 64 of this Act, and is not itself in reversion expectant (whether immediately or not) on an interest which fulfils those conditions.

(1A)   The reference in subsection (1) above to a person who is the owner of an interest such as is mentioned in that subsection is to be construed, where different persons own such interests in different parts of the property, as a reference to all those persons collectively.

(2)   References in this Part of this Act to a notice to quit given by the landlord are references to a notice to quit given by the immediate landlord.

(3)   The provisions of the Sixth Schedule to this Act shall have effect for the application of this Part of this Act to cases where the immediate landlord of the tenant is not the owner of the fee simple in respect of the holding.

45 . . .

. . .

46 Interpretation of Part II

(1)   In this Part of this Act:–

'business' has the meaning assigned to it by subsection (2) of section 23 of this Act;

'current tenancy' means the tenancy under which the tenant holds for the time being;

'date of termination' has the meaning assigned to it by subsection (1) of section 25 of this Act;

subject to the provisions of section 32 of this Act, 'the holding' has the meaning assigned to it by subsection (3) of section 23 of this Act;

'interim rent' has the meaning given by section 24A(1) of this Act;

'mining lease' has the same meaning as in the Landlord and Tenant Act 1927.

(2)   For the purposes of this Part of this Act, a person has a controlling interest in a company, if, had he been a company, the other company would have been its subsidiary; and in this Part–

'company' has the meaning given by section 735 of the Companies Act 1985; and

'subsidiary' has the meaning given by section 736 of that Act.

INDEX

References are to paragraph numbers

Agricultural holdings   1.5
Alienation
    assignment. *See* Assignment
    new leases   5.8
    and telecommunications
        agreements   12.6
Alterations
    new leases   5.7, 5.9
    Telecommunications Code   12.4
Alternative accommodation   4.1
Alternative dispute resolution   6.12
Appeals, orders for new tenancies
    6.11
Assignment
    1995 Act   5.8
    conditions   5.8
    grounds for withholding consent
        5.8
    guarantees   5.8
    inter-group assignment   5.8, 8.9
    new leases   5.8
    partnerships   2.11
    unlawful assignment   2.9
Association of British Insurers   5.8

Breach of statutory duty   2.2
Break clauses
    new leases   5.3
    and redevelopment   5.3
    and s.25 notices   2.3
    and s.26 requests   3.3
    telecommunications agreements
        12.6
Break notices   2.3
Business occupancy   1.4, 10.2
Business tenancies
    Code of Practice   5.2, 5.8
    excluded tenancies   1.5
    meaning   1.4, 10.2

security of tenure   1.1, 1.3
termination. *See* Termination of
    tenancies
transitional provisions   1.2

Calderbank letters   6.9
Capital gains tax   10.4
Code of Practice for Commercial
    Leases   5.2, 5.8
Companies
    group companies
        inter-group assignment   5.8, 8.9
        objections to renewal   4.3
    group occupation   2.10
    service of notices to   2.7
Compensation
    14-year rule   10.2
    calculation   10.2
    contracting out   10.6
    entitlement   10.1
    flowchart   10.2
    generally   10.1–10.6
    improvements   3.6, 3.7, 11.3
    misrepresentation   10.5
    multiple grounds   10.1
    rating revaluations   10.3
    taxation   10.4
    telecommunications agreements
        12.6
    unlawful assignment   2.9
Contracting out
    compensation provisions   10.6
    renewal provisions   1.6
Costs. *See* Legal costs
County courts
    interim rent applications   6.6
    jurisdiction   6.2, 6.3
Court applications
    application procedure   6.4

Court applications – *cont*
  Calderbank letters   6.9
  case management   6.1
    alternative dispute resolution
      6.12
    directions   6.8
    hearings   6.7
  Civil Procedure Rules   6.1
  claim forms   6.41
  copies   6.4
  costs   6.9, 6.10
  documents   6.8
  first hearings   6.7
  generally   6.1–6.12
  human right   6.8
  interim rents   6.6
  issuing   6.4
  jurisdiction
    determination of county court
      6.3
    High Court or county court   6.2
  landlords' applications   2.5, 3.1
  legislative changes   6.1
  listing questionnaires   6.8
  orders
    for new tenancies   6.11
    telecommunications agreements
      12.2, 12.3
  pre-action protocols   6.1
  response procedure   6.5
  service
    acknowledgements   6.5
    procedure   6.4
  settlement offers   6.9
  statements of truth   6.4
  stay of proceedings, ADR   6.12
  tenants' applications   3.1, 3.4
  time limits   3.5, 6.1
    extension   3.5
    post s.26 requests   3.7
  timing   2.3, 2.4
  withdrawal of proceedings   2.5, 7.5,
    7.7
Covenants
  breach, termination ground   4.1
  consent to assignment   5.8
  telecommunications agreements
    12.6

Defects, s.25 notices   2.6, 3.8
Demolition. *See* Redevelopment
Development. *See* Redevelopment
Dilapidations
  claims   9.1
  discontinuance of renewal
    proceedings   7.8
  forfeiture for disrepair   9.4
  generally   9.1–9.4
  new leases   5.7
  options   9.1
  and redevelopment intentions   9.2
  service charge trap   9.3
Discontinuance notices   7.7

Errors
  counternotices   3.4
  procedural errors   3.5
  section 25 notices   2.3, 2.6
Estoppel   2.6, 3.4, 3.5, 3.8
Expert evidence, new rents   5.5

Forfeiture
  disrepair   9.4
  telecommunications agreements
    12.5, 12.6

Goodwill   5.5
Guarantees
  assignment   5.8
  new leases   5.4

High Court, jurisdiction   6.2
Human rights, and court
  applications   6.8

Improvements
  compensation   11.3
  compensation claims   3.6
    time limits   3.6, 3.7
  court applications   11.2
  effect on new rents   5.5

Improvements – *cont*
  notices   11.2
  objection notices   11.2
  procedure   11.2
  and rent reviews   5.6
  tenants' rights to carry out   11.1
Insolvency, landlords   2.12
Insurance
  new leases   5.9
  telecommunications operators
    12.6
  uninsured risks   5.9
Interest, new leases   5.9
Interim rents
  advice to landlords   8.9
  applications
    county court procedure   6.6
    old and new law   6.6
    withdrawal   8.6
  competent applicants   2.8, 3.2, 8.2,
    8.3
  discontinuance of proceedings   7.7
  generally   8.1–8.10
  new law   2.1
    calculation principles   8.7
    commencement   8.3
    competent applicants   8.3
    and last day rent reviews   8.8
  and objections to renewal   8.7
  old law
    calculation principles   8.4
    commencement   8.2, 8.3
    competent applicants   8.2
    county court cases   8.4
    discounts   8.4
    landlords' options   8.6
    timing of applications   8.2
  origins   8.1
  rising and falling markets   8.5
  time limits   2.3

Keep open clauses   5.9

Landlord occupation
  5 year-rule   2.4, 4.3
  compensation to tenants   10.1
  group companies   4.3

  intentions   4.3
  part occupation   4.3
  real possibility   4.3
  requirements for termination   4.3
  termination ground   4.1
Landlords
  and assignment clauses   5.8
  competent landlords   2.2, 2.8, 3.2
  goodwill   7.7
  initial considerations   2.1
  insolvency   2.12
  and interim rents   8.6, 8.9
  new options   2.5
  notices. *See* Section 40 notices
  objections. *See* Termination grounds
  occupation of tenancies. *See* Landlord
    occupation
  position   2.1–2.11
  reversionary interests   2.8
  tactics   2.4
  timetables   App 2
  timing   2.4
Leases
  new leases. *See* New leases
  registration   3.9
Legal costs
  choice of court   6.2
  court applications   6.10
  discontinuance of proceedings by
    tenants   7.7
  new leases   5.10
  and offers to settle   6.9, 6.10
Licences   1.4
Liquidation, landlords   2.12

Mining leases   1.5
Misrepresentation
  competency as landlords   2.8
  termination grounds   10.5

New leases
  1995 Act, impact   5.8
  alienation   5.8
  alterations   5.7, 5.9
  break clauses   5.3
  commencement   5.9
  consent to assignment   5.8

New leases – *cont*
  court orders for   6.11
    appeals   6.11
    duration   5.3, 5.9
    essential terms for tenants   5.9
    extent of property   5.1
    generally   5.1–5.10
    guarantors   5.4
    initial rents   5.5, 5.9
    insurance   5.9
    interest   5.9
    keep open clauses   5.9
    legal costs   5.10
    maximum duration   5.3
    permitted uses   5.9
    reinstatement   5.7
    rent reviews   5.6, 5.9
    repairs   5.7
    service charges   5.9
    short leases   5.3
    uninsured risks   5.9
    variation of terms   5.2
Notices to quit
  by tenants   3.3, 7.2, 7.4, 7.6
  definition   3.3

Offers of settlement   6.9
Orders
  new tenancies   2.2
  telecommunications agreements
    12.2, 12.3
Overriding interests   3.9

Part 36 offers   6.9
Partnerships   2.11
Pending land actions   3.9
Planning permissions, applications
    2.4
Practice directions   6.1
Professional Arbitration on Court Terms
    (PACT)   6.12
Property Litigation Association   6.8

Quarter days   7.4

Rating revaluations   10.3
Receivership, landlords   2.12

Reconstruction. *See* Redevelopment
Redevelopment
  and break clauses   5.3
  burden of proof   2.4, 4.2
  compensation to tenants   10.1
  intentions   4.2
  requirements   4.2
  short new leases   5.3
  and Telecommunications Code
    12.4
  termination ground   4.1
Reinstatement
  new leases   5.7
  Telecommunications Code   12.4
Renewal
  new leases. *See* New leases
  objections. *See* Termination grounds
  requests. *See* Section 26 requests
Rent reviews
  last day rent reviews   8.8
  new leases   5.6, 5.9
  telecommunications agreements
    12.6
Rents
  arrears   4.1, 5.8
  discontinuance of proceedings   7.7
  interim. *See* Interim rents
  new leases
    disregards   5.5
    expert evidence   5.5
    initial rents   5.5, 5.9
  passing rent and market rents   2.1,
    3.2, 8.3
Repairs
  dilapidations   9.1–4
  new leases   5.7
  termination ground   4.1
Reversionary interests   2.8, 5.8

Section 25 notices
  amendment   2.6
  and break clauses   2.3
  challenges   2.6, 3.8
    new notices   2.6
  checklists   App 3
  competent landlords   2.2, 2.8
  contents   2.3

Section 25 notices – *cont*
  counternotices   3.4, 3.8
  defects   2.6
    tenants' responses   3.8
  errors   2.3, 2.6
  forms   2.3, App 1
  interim rents   2.1, 2.3
  service   2.7
  tenants' considerations   3.4
  termination dates   2.3
    invalid dates   2.6
  time limits   2.3
    tenants' checklist   3.6
  transitional provisions   1.2
  validity   2.6, 3.8
  withdrawal   2.6
Section 26 requests
  and break clauses   3.3
  checklists   App 3
  competent landlords   3.2
  contents   3.1
  counternotices   3.1
    form   App 1
    time limits   3.7
  delay   3.2
  effect   3.2
  form   3.1, App 1
  interim rents   2.1
  service   3.1, 3.8
  and tenants' intentions   10.1
  timing   2.4, 3.1, 3.2
    post-request checklist   3.7
  transitional provisions   1.2
  withdrawal of proceedings   7.3
Section 40 notices
  breach of statutory duty   2.2
  contents   2.2
  failing to answer   2.2
  form   App 1
  incorrect information   2.2
  time limits   2.2, 2.4
  timing   2.4
  use by tenants   3.2
Section 146 notices   9.4
Security of tenure
  business tenancies   1.1, 1.3
  contracting out   1.6
  telecommunication installations
    12.6

Service
  court applications   6.4
  methods   6.4
  recorded delivery   2.7
  s.25 notices   2.7
  s.26 requests   3.1, 3.8
Service charges
  and dilapidations claims   9.3
  new leases   5.9
  service charge trap   9.3
Service tenancies   1.5
Short leases   1.5, 5.3
Solicitors, negligence   3.5
Statements of truth   6.4
Statutory duty, breach   2.2
Subsidiaries, definition   2.10
Sub-tenants
  group companies   2.10
  information to landlords   2.2
  section 40 notices to   2.4
  termination ground   4.1
    compensation   10.1
  timetables   App 2

Tactics
  landlords   2.4
  tenants   3.2
Taxation, compensation   10.4
Telecommunications Code
  advice to occupiers   12.6
  advice to operators   12.5
  agreements   12.2, 12.3, 12.5, 12.6
  alterations   12.4
  and change of use   12.4
  compulsory purchase effect   12.1,
    12.3
  conditions of application   12.2
  court orders   12.2, 12.3
  and development   12.4
  generally   12.1–12.6
  legal status   12.1
  operators' rights   12.3
  reinstatement   12.4
  removal of apparatus   12.4
Tenancies at will   1.5
Tenants
  and assignment clauses   5.8

Tenants – *cont*
  company groups   2.10
  compensation to. *See* Compensation
  considerations   3.1–9
  interim rent applications   8.3, 8.9
  meaning   2.9
  new options   3.4
  partnerships   2.11
  renewal requests. *See* Section 26
    requests
  and s.25 notices   3.4
  tactics   3.2, 3.8
  time limits   3.5
    checklist   3.6
  timetables   App 2
  trustees   2.10
  unlawful assignment   2.9
Termination dates
  effect of s. 26 requests   3.1
  landlords' considerations   2.3
  landlords' tactics   2.4
  new options   2.5
  validity   2.6
Termination grounds
  counternotices   3.1
  and interim rents   8.7
  landlords' considerations   2.1
  misrepresentations   10.5
  new options   2.5
  permitted grounds   1.3
    generally   4.1
    multiple grounds   2.6
  section 25 notices   2.3
  specification   2.3
    court procedures   6.5

Termination of tenancies
  court applications   6.4
    responses   6.5
  discontinuance of proceedings
    7.5, 7.7
  generally   7.1–7.8
  grounds. *See* Termination grounds
  methods   1.3
  surrender by operation of law   7.6
  tenants leaving   7.1
  tenants' notices to quit   7.2
    after expiry dates   7.6
    effect   3.3
    quarter days   7.4
  timetables   App 2
  walking away after expiry date   7.6
  withdrawal prior to proceedings
    7.3
Termination orders, applications   2.5
Time
  calculation   2.3
  landlords' tactics   2.4
  section 25 notices   2.3
  tenants' time limits   3.5
    checklist   3.6
    post-s.26 requests   3.7
Transitional provisions   1.2
Trustees, tenants   2.10

Use
  change of use   12.4
  permitted use   5.9

Value added tax   10.4